Norman T. Carrington MA

Brodie's Notes on William Shakespeare's

Macbeth

Pan Educational London and Sydney

First published 1948 by James Brodie Ltd,
[illegible] Bath BA1 2HW
This edition published [illegible] by Pan Books Ltd,
[illegible] 9PG

ISBN 0 330 50002 3
Printed and bound in Great Britain by
Richard Clay (The Chaucer Press) Ltd, Bungay, Suffolk

Contents

The author

Surprisingly little is known of the life of our greatest dramatist, and the little we know is derived mainly from brief references to his name in legal and other formal documents. He was born in Stratford-on-Avon, and, although the exact date of his birth is unknown, there is a record that he was christened William on 26 April 1564, the third child (and eldest son) of John Shakespeare, a man variously described as glover, wool-dealer, farmer, and butcher. Until about the year 1578, when his business seems to have begun to decline, John Shakespeare was a notable figure in Stratford, and it is probable that William was educated at Stratford Grammar School, where he may have learned the 'small Latin and less Greek' for which Jonson gave him credit. However this may be, the next thing we know that can be accepted as reliable is that at the end of 1582, at the age of eighteen, he married Anne Hathaway, a woman eight years older than himself, and that by 1585 three children had been born of the marriage. In this year he is thought to have left Stratford for London. Tradition has it that his departure was owing to trouble over deer-stealing in the grounds of Sir Thomas Lucy, but in the light of modern research it would appear that he left with a band of strolling players, the Queen's Players, who visited Stratford in 1585.

Whether his wife and children ever lived with him in London is not known, but it is unlikely; nor do we know what he himself did there before 1592, but from a pamphlet published in that year by Robert Greene, a lesser dramatist, we have news of him as actor and playwright. Plague caused the theatres to be closed in 1593, and on their re-opening in the following year we know that Shakespeare was a member of the Lord Chamberlain's Company (known, after the accession of James I, as the King's Men), and it is probable that he stayed with this company for the remainder of his career, writing plays for it and acting with it in various theatres. His connection with the company must have brought him considerable financial reward, for we know that in 1596 his father, presumably aided by his successful son, applied to the College of Heralds for the right to assume a family coat of arms, and in the following year the playwright purchased (for £60!) New Place, one of the largest houses in Stratford. Although the house is no longer there, the foundations can be seen and the garden is open to the public. As his fortunes prospered, Shakespeare bought shares in two theatres, the Globe, built in 1599, and the Blackfriars, built in 1609, so that, in addition to his pay as actor and writer, he would receive his share of the profits on these investments.

Thus in 1611, when still under fifty years of age, Shakespeare retired to his native town, a fairly wealthy man, though he seems to have kept up a connection with London, as he was concerned in a legal dispute over the purchase of a house in Blackfriars in 1615. He died in Stratford-on-Avon, survived by his wife and two daughters, on 23 April 1616, and was buried in the Parish Church, where thousands of people from all over the world visit his grave every year.

As an actor Shakespeare does not seem to have been eminent, but even in his own day his fame as a dramatist was very great. Thus Meres in 1598 described him as 'the most excellent in both kinds' (i.e. in comedy and in tragedy) and even Ben Jonson, whose dramatic work was in a very different vein from that of Shakespeare, remarks in his *Discoveries*, 'I lov'd the man and do honour his memory (on this side idolatry) as much as any'.

Shakespeare probably began his work as a dramatist by collaborating with others and patching up old plays which his company wished to revive. His first completely original play is believed to be *Love's Labour's Lost* (1591 ?), though the date of each play is itself a problem, since the dates are not given in the First Folio (the first collected edition of his plays, 1623). His non-dramatic works consist of two narrative poems, *Venus and Adonis* (1593) and *The Rape of Lucrece* (1594), and the one hundred and fifty-four sonnets published in 1609 – without Shakespeare's permission it is thought. The first one hundred and twenty-six of the sonnets are addressed to a young man, the poet's friend and patron; the remainder to a 'dark lady', and the identity of neither of these two is established, nor is it decided how far, if at all, the series may be considered autobiographical. Most of Shakespeare's plays were written for performance in the public playhouses, and they were conveniently classified in the First Folio in three groups – comedies, histories and tragedies. But when considered chronologically they seem to fall naturally into four periods, thus admirably described by Professor Dowden.

> First, from about 1590 to 1595–96, years of dramatic apprenticeship and experiment; secondly, from about 1595–96 to about 1600–01, the period of the English historical plays and the mirthful and joyous comedies; thirdly, from 1601 to about 1608, the period of grave and bitter comedies and of the great tragedies; last, from about 1608 to 1611 or 1613, the period of the romantic plays, which are at once grave and glad, serene and beautiful.

Professor Dowden names these periods respectively 'In the workshop', 'In the world', 'Out of the depths', 'On the heights'. *Macbeth* belongs to the period of the great tragedies, and all the evidence points to 1606 as the date of its composition. The great tragedies were *Othello*, *King Lear*, *Macbeth*, *Antony and Cleopatra* and *Coriolanus* in that order, and those who know these plays can only stand amazed at the fullness and the power and the penetration of this man's mind, and honour his memory in just measure, as it was honoured all over the world in the quatercentenary celebrations of his birth. *Macbeth* is a popular play and is often played. At the end of 1967 a celebrity audience, including a former Soviet president and the world's first spaceman, gave the Royal Shakespeare Company a ten minute ovation after a performance of *Macbeth* in Moscow. Students unable to see a live performance may like to know that there is a recording (a straight reproduction) on sale.

The play

Plot

Macbeth and Banquo are returning from crushing the rebellion of the Thane of Cawdor against King Duncan of Scotland, when they are met by three witches who greet Macbeth as Thane of Cawdor and king thereafter, and prophesy that Banquo shall be father to a line of kings. Hardly have the words left their lips when messengers come to tell Macbeth that the King has created him Thane of Cawdor as a reward for his services.

The King honours Macbeth by coming to stay at his castle. There, at the instigation of his wife, Macbeth murders him and seizes the crown.

In view of the witches' prophecy concerning Banquo, Macbeth tries to make himself sure on the throne by plotting the death of Banquo and his son, Fleance. The ruffians he hires are successful in murdering Banquo, but Fleance escapes.

Macbeth now seeks out the witches, who bid him beware of Macduff and give him a sense of security by telling him that none of woman born shall harm him and that he shall never be vanquished till Birnam wood move to Dunsinane hill.

Macduff makes good his escape before Macbeth can implement the witches' warning, and in sheer spite Macbeth has his wife and children slaughtered. The effects of his murders and misrule are now seen in the forces gathering head against him, and at the end he is defeated and killed, and yet the letter of the prophecies remains unbroken.

The absence of sub-plot gives a sense of rapidity to the action. (This is further helped by the fact that there are only two main characters.)

Macbeth has always been a popular play with all classes of playgoers: those who seek in the drama 'the mirror of nature' find a page of the book of life writ large, and those who crave blood and violence get fights and murders galore, to say nothing of witchcraft.

Source of plot and its treatment

The story is taken from Holinshed's *Chronicles of England, Scot-*

land and Ireland. The following are Shakespeare's chief alterations, all for a dramatic purpose.

1 Two battles against the rebels are combined into one. Obviously duplication on the stage would be monotonous. Similarly it took two battles to displace Macbeth, which Shakespeare concentrates into one.

2 Malcolm is named as Duncan's heir earlier, so as to give Macbeth reason for taking things into his own hands at once and not leaving them to chance.

3 Macbeth is made to be Duncan's host at the time he murders him, thus making the crime seem more heinous and increasing our sympathy for the unsuspecting Duncan.

4 Duncan is represented as a good king, whereas really he was as big a villain as Macbeth. This again has the effect of increasing our sympathy for him. If his character in the play were as in history we should regard his murder as a blessing and Macbeth as a deliverer.

5 Instead of meeting, on three different occasions, 'weird sisters', 'wizzards' and 'a certeine witch', in the play Macbeth meets the same 'weird sisters' (twice). This gives concentration of character interest as **1** does of events.

Of course, there is nothing in Holinshed of Shakespeare's characterization. A mere succession of events becomes a story with cause and effect, *due to human character*. Macbeth himself is responsible for the ruin of his soul. The same bricks and mortar as Holinshed, but what different architecture! A story which in Holinshed's hands is crude and improbable becomes real and lifelike and moves us because we feel our kinship with the actors.

Theme

The theme of *Macbeth* is

> Vaulting ambition, which o'erleaps itself
> And falls on the other (I. vii. 27–8).

With every murder Macbeth thinks that he will have gained his object and it will be the last. But he still has his ambition.

Having obtained the crown, he is further ambitious to keep it in his own family. Surely, just one more murder will give him all he wants. And so it goes on. 'Though ye take from a covetous man all his treasure', says Milton, 'he has yet one jewel left; ye cannot deprive him of his covetousness.'

Macbeth has no sooner sinned than he loses joy of the fruits of his sin: the happiness he had looked for gets farther and farther away as each new crime increases his remorse and fear.

Shakespearian tragedy goes down to the root of things. The struggle in Macbeth is a symbol of the struggle between good and evil in men. And goodness and evil each brings its own reward. As Tennyson says,

> And, because right is right, to follow right
> Were wisdom in the scorn of consequence.

Setting

The great majority of Shakespeare's plays, apart from the English Histories, are set in places abroad, a device which of itself gave them a romantic colouring.

The local colour of all Shakespeare's plays is that of Elizabethan England, whether the story is one of Scotland, Denmark or Italy, and in whatever age. Nowadays we should demand strict accuracy in scenery, costume and topical references, but then, for playwright and audience alike, the life and spirit of a play mattered more than strict accuracy in local colour. 'It is the spirit which giveth life.' People saw in the drama a reflection of their own life and experience; its appeal was in no wise analytical or educational, but human.

Further, in those days people were untravelled and uneducated, and anachronisms would not strike a false note in an age more familiar with the stories than with the settings.

And it must be remembered that there was no scenery and the vaguest period costume. Incongruities which become apparent beside 'realistic' scenery would not be noticed then. In references to a character's dress it would be farcical were the references historically correct but to something the character was not actually wearing on the stage!

Macbeth takes place nominally in Scotland in the eleventh century, but we are really never very far from the England

Shakespeare knew. We hear of 'cannons' (I. ii. 37), and at the beginning of Act II Fleance is waiting for 'the clock' to strike, and Macbeth's castle (with 'jutty, frieze, buttress' and 'coign of vantage') is not unlike the castles Shakespeare had seen in Warwickshire (to say nothing of the porter!). Everyone in the audience would have been to fairs where 'rarer monsters' were 'painted upon a pole' and, in a bear-baiting age, would be familiar with a bear tied to a stake. The King of England cures 'the evil' as James I did (IV. iii. 141–51), and the union of the crowns of England and Scotland under James I is referred to in IV. i. 120–2. At the time of *Macbeth* James I was still very popular. He was also very interested in witchcraft. Such topical references are indicated in the notes.

Characters

Macbeth is such a short and concentrated play, with only two main characters, that it has been thought better to follow the development of the characters of Macbeth and Lady Macbeth scene by scene through the play, instead of by separate character-studies as in the other plays in these Notes.

For the sake of convenience features in which they can be contrasted are here set out.

The nature of their ambition. – Macbeth for himself, Lady Macbeth for her husband. She has no personal ambition.

The nature of their courage. – Macbeth has physical courage in a right cause; Lady Macbeth has complete disregard of consequences. See also pp.17, 56, 59, 63 and below.

The nature of their self-delusion. – That just one more murder will give them what they want. cf. also their euphemisms.

Imagination. See pp.27, 33 (note on 'What do you mean?'), 56.

Conscience. See pp.24-5, 30, 32, 63 and below. Lady Macbeth has conscience, but suppresses it (see pp.24-5).

Will-power and self-reliance. – Lady Macbeth is the firmer; Macbeth is more unsettled by mental worries. See pp.24-5, 56.

Intellect. – Here there is little to choose between them.

Superstition.
Suspicion. } Macbeth's the greater.

Affection (a) for each other – Lady Macbeth loves Macbeth well (see pp.25, 43); (b) for their country – Macbeth's is strong at first, but as the play proceeds he more and more uses his country for his own advancement. Lady Macbeth is not concerned with the good of Scotland.

The good in each, e.g. Macbeth's courage and Lady Macbeth's concern for her husband.

Analysis of the growth of Macbeth's remorse and fear

Remorse and fear of the consequences are naturally reciprocal.

What remorse there is shows that there was some goodness in Macbeth.

Macbeth has no fear of physical terrors, e.g. the battle and 'What man dare I dare' (III. iv. 99ff.). 'Horrible imaginings' cause his fear. See Lady Macbeth's masterly analysis of his character.

> Thou 'ldst have, great Glamis,
> That which cries 'Thus must thou do, if thou have it';
> And that which rather thou dost fear to do
> Than wishest should be undone.

Duncan's murder

Meditation beforehand

Soliloquy, I. vii. Fear of the immediate consequences is most prominent.

Hallucination of the dagger.

After the murder

> Wherefore could not I pronounce 'Amen'?
> I had most need of blessing.
> I am afraid to think what I have done.
> Every noise appals me.
> Wake Duncan with thy knocking! I would thou couldst!

Banquo's murder

Meditation beforehand

> Our fears in Banquo stick deep (III. i. 49ff.)
> For Banquo's issue have I filed my mind;
> Put rancours in the vessel of my peace.

> Ere we will eat our meal in fear, and sleep
> In the affliction of these terrible dreams
> That shake us nightly.

Macbeth kills Banquo to avoid 'The torture of the mind', thereby *increasing* his fear (owing to the power of his imagination).

His hiring of ruffians to do this and the following murder shows his fear of a recurrence of his experiences when he murdered Duncan.

After the murder

'Saucy doubts and fears' when Fleance has escaped.

Hallucination. (N.B. Not until *after* the murder.) His cheek is 'blanch'd with fear' when the Ghost comes, yet the Russian bear or the Hyrcan tiger would not fright him.

'Thou canst not say I did it' – fear of consequences.

The murder of Lady Macduff and her children

Meditation beforehand

Reflection on his fears, and an attempt to deaden them by habit – 'The initiate fear that wants hard use'.

> Strange things I have in head, that will to hand;
> Which must be acted ere they may be scann'd.

If he waits to consider what he intends, fear (or his better nature) would restrain him.

His fear of the uncertain future causes him to consult the witches. After saying, previously, 'There is none but he [Banquo] whose being I do fear', he shows fear of Macduff – 'Thou hast harp'd my fear aright'.

> Thou shalt not live;
> That I may tell pale-hearted fear it lies.

After the murder

Neither remorse nor fear. For a time his sensibilities are deadened.

No hallucination, either before or after the murder.

At the end of the play,

> My soul is too much charged
> With blood of thine already.

Style

Professor Dowden has an excellent summary of the development of Shakespeare's style.

> In the earliest plays the language is sometimes as it were a dress put upon the thought – a dress ornamented with superfluous care; the idea is at times hardly sufficient to fill out the language in which it is put; in the middle of plays (*Julius Cæsar* serves as an example) there seems a perfect balance and equality between the thought and its expression. In the latest plays this balance is disturbed by the preponderance or excess of the ideas over the means of giving them utterance. The sentences are close-packed; there are 'rapid and abrupt turnings of thought, so quick that language can hardly follow fast enough; impatient activity of intellect and fancy, which, having once disclosed an idea, cannot wait to work it orderly out'; 'the language is sometimes alive with imagery'.

Macbeth is typical of the latest plays. Shakespeare often expresses more in a sentence than seems possible. Graphic and figurative language abounds, and the vividness and variety of the imagery is to be noted. There is quick change of metaphor, though without confusion, as the metaphors are usually connected, or naturally combined in one conception, as, for instance, in Macbeth's soliloquy, I. vii. 21–8, or his words on sleep to Lady Macbeth, II. ii. 7–40. The metaphors invariably have a sense of vitality and freshness about them, and that sense of surprise and yet of fitness which characterizes the metaphors of a genius. An instance of a mixed metaphor is I. vii. 36, where the metaphor 'dress'd', although carrying on the metaphor of the previous speech, 'which would be worn now in their newest gloss', does not fit in with its accompanying metaphors.

The close-packed, elliptical style of many speeches in *Macbeth* is inferior dramatically, as it is difficult to understand the thought at the speed at which the words are spoken. But the *form* of Shakespeare's mature verse is dramatically far superior. His verse is very free, making the dialogue more natural and more adapted to different characters. Many lines are 'run-on', that is, the sense of one line is completed in the next and there is no stop at the end of the line; the stronger pauses are placed within the line at different points; many lines have extra und syllables. It would be futile to give examples when all longer speeches of the main characters are typical of Shakespeare's later style.

In a good play the style naturally reflects the character of the person speaking, and even the same person in two different moods may speak in two different ways. Look at Macbeth's abrupt and disjointed speeches when he is desperate in Act V and contrast them with his speeches in the early part of the play.

In *Macbeth* Shakespeare makes full use of dramatic irony – the difference between the situation as known to the audience and as supposed by the characters of the play (or by some of them). The basis of dramatic irony is ambiguity of meaning. A remark by one character may have a surface meaning for the other characters in the play but an additional significance for the audience. In *Macbeth* dramatic irony usually springs from the ignorance of Macbeth and Lady Macbeth of coming events. Particular examples are pointed out in the textual notes, e.g. p.23.

Notice the little circumstantial details that give the truth of fact to the fiction of the play, e.g. 'at the south entry', 'till the second cock', 'on Tuesday last', 'till seven at night', 'almost a mile' – and the student will readily find others for himself.

The normal line in Shakespeare's plays is a blank verse iambic pentameter, but the witches speak in a rhyming trochaic tetrameter. The effect of this is to differentiate their speech from that of the ordinary mortals in the play, giving it the 'ring' of a chant. The verse chimes with their rites and riddles.

When prose is used it is for a definite purpose. Prose is invariably used for comic characters (e.g. the porter, II. iii.) and characters of lower social position (e.g. the doctor and the gentlewoman, V. i). This was a literary convention at a time when literature was aristocratic and the chief characters in plays (as in life) were kings and nobles. Scenes in which the lower orders of society figure are a contrast; these people live on a lower plane of feeling than the main characters, and thereby emphasize the height of the feeling of the main characters, and the contrast in the medium of expression – prose instead of verse – is in perfect keeping.

When Lady Macbeth talks in her sleep (V. i.) prose is the

medium. Prose, especially the broken prose Shakespeare uses, expresses her distracted state of mind much better than verse, which would be too beautiful, smooth and regular for such 'slumbery agitation'.

Prose is also used for the talk of Lady Macduff and her son, Act IV Scene ii. This is a homely scene, contrasting with the high tragedy with which it is surrounded, and the difference is emphasised by the difference in form. Verse, again, would seem too dignified and regular for this unaffected childish prattle.

Macbeth's letter (I. v.) is obviously in prose.

The Elizabethan theatre

At the time of Shakespeare there were probably not more than five public theatres in the land, all in London, and they were built according to the design of the inn-yards of the period, which had been found marvellously convenient places for the presentation of plays.

The theatre was circular or octagonal in shape. The main part of the auditorium was the large round pit, open to the sky, in which the poorer people *stood* (the 'groundlings'). Encircling this, round the walls, were three balconies, covered on top but not in front (like the 'stands' on a football ground), and containing seats. The price of admission to the pit was one penny, equivalent to about fifteen pence nowadays and balcony seats ranged from twopence to half-a-crown, according to their position. When it was wet the performance was postponed until the next day.

The stage was large, jutting far into the pit, and was without scenery and any but the most meagre properties. Hence it made no difference that people stood at the side of the stage as well as in front. Scenery and atmospheric conditions were created in the imagination of the audience by the words of the characters in the play: they were made part of the play, so as not to obtrude and destroy the illusion of reality, as, for example, in *Macbeth* at the beginning of I. vi and II. i, and III. ii 50–2. *Macbeth,* it has to be remembered, would be performed in broad daylight, and the references to the blackness of the night have an imaginative effect.

The play went straight on without intervals. Lack of intervals and frequent changes of scene were immaterial when the stage was without scenery, consequently a succession of short scenes, as in Act V, is quite common in Elizabethan drama. It should be remembered that on Shakespeare's stage there were no separate scenes *as such.* In the early part of the present century his plays were presented with elaborate, often spectacular, scenery, and sometimes the audience would become impatient at the constant delays while it was being changed. At the present time there is a return to a simple stage setting, in keeping with that of Shakespeare's day, as, for instance, at the Royal Shakespeare Theatre, Stratford-on-Avon. There is good reason to believe

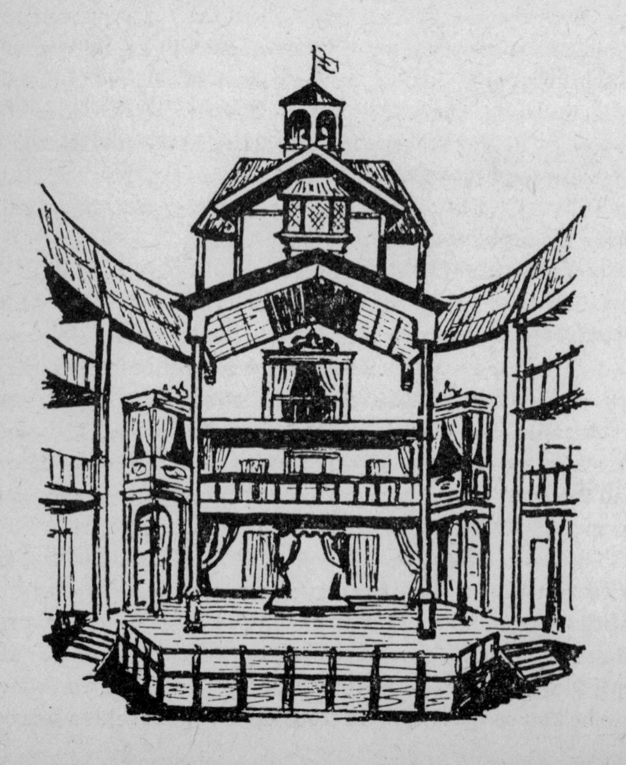

that when they were first produced the plays took considerably less time than they do today. The Prologue to *Romeo and Juliet*, for example, refers to 'the two hours' traffic of our stage'.

The end of a scene was frequently marked by rhyming lines, as in Act I Scenes i, ii, iv at Macbeth's exit, v and vii. Just as the scenery had to be *put into* the play, so had entrances and exits to be arranged as *part of* the play. In a modern play an actor can get into position before the rise of the curtain, but on the open stage it would seem artificial if he walked on and then started his first speech, or finished the scene and then walked off. Such endings as I. iii, 'Come friends'; iv, 'Let's after him'; vi, 'Conduct me to mine host'; vii, 'Away', clear the stage and at the same time fit in perfectly naturally with the play. It follows that 'dead' bodies always had to be carried off the stage in the action of the play.

It was not unknown for the stage floor to be equipped with a trap door for the sudden appearance and disappearance of ghosts and spirits, and some theatres had a flying apparatus by which such could descend on the stage with the aid of ropes on runners. Under the stage was an orchestra, a very important feature of the Elizabethan theatre. There is not much scope for music in a dire play like *Macbeth*, but oboes are specified, drums are called for with marching soldiers and music with song or dance in association with the witches.

At the back of the stage was a recess ('within'), and this was curtained and could be shut off when desired. The 'within' would, no doubt, serve for the witches' cavern in Act IV Scene i. Above the recess was a balcony, which served for castle walls, an upper room and suchlike scenes. It appears that this too could be curtained off. People seem to have been fond of balcony scenes, particularly when there was an escape from the balcony – an upper room, for example – to the main stage – representing the ground below. There are none, however, in *Macbeth*.

People who wanted to be in the public eye were able to hire stools actually on the stage itself. Payment of one shilling extra entitled them to have their pipes lit by a page, thus showing to all and sundry that they were in a position to be attended. Such a privilege would be valued by country gentlemen who wanted it to be known that they had come up to town. It was a source of

continual annoyance to playwrights that actors 'gagged' in order to please these aristocratic playgoers.

No women were allowed to act by law. Consequently women's parts were taken by boys with unbroken voices. Imagine a boy's rendering of Lady Macbeth or of Imogen or Cleopatra! This accounts for the few women's parts in plays of the period, though some were always introduced for the sake of variety. It also accounts for the large number of plays where a woman disguises herself as a page boy. It made it much easier for the producer; further, the audience was intrigued by a situation in which a character was pretending to be what he really was! In *The Merchant of Venice* every one of the female characters takes on male disguise.

Plays were not acted in period costume, though frequently *some* attempt was made to suggest a period, and the result must often have been a bizarre compromise. Thus all Shakespeare's plays can be said to have been first acted in 'modern dress'. Although there was no scenery, managers spared no expense on the most lavish of costumes.

On days when the theatre was open a flag was flown from the turret, and when the play was about to begin a trumpet was sounded. The turret of the Globe Theatre, the best remembered of all the early theatres, housed a big alarum bell, a favourite theatrical effect. Shakespeare may have been thinking of this bell when he makes Macduff shout, 'Ring the alarum-bell'.

Teachers will find Brodie's Filmstrip *The Theatre in Shakespeare's Day* helpful in presenting the theatre of *Macbeth* more vividly.

One must not imagine that it was difficult for Shakespeare to write plays for such a theatre. It would have been difficult for him to write for any other than the one to which he was accustomed. What we have never known we can never miss.

The text of Shakespeare's plays

Few readers of Shakespeare realize the difficulties scholars have had to overcome in order to establish accurate texts of the plays. The First Folio (see p.vi) contained thirty-six plays. This is the basis of all subsequent editions. Other large-size collected editions or Folios were published in the seventeenth century, the Third and Fourth Folios containing seven additional plays, none of which, with the exception of *Pericles*, is now thought to be by Shakespeare. Sixteen of the plays had already been published separately as Quartos (editions half folio size) before 1623, and in the case of some plays, for example, *Hamlet*, more than one Quarto edition exists. Some of these Quartos are almost word for word the same as the texts in the First Folio and were possibly set up from Shakespeare's own manuscript or at least from accurate theatre copies; but others are shortened, inferior versions, possibly 'pirated' editions published by some unauthorized person who had access to theatre copies or parts of them, or who had taken down the plays in shorthand while they were being performed. It is thought that the texts of the First Folio were set up from the good Quartos and from good theatre copies. But these texts must all be compared, printers' mistakes and other interference traced, before a reliable text can be arrived at. The first editor to attempt the problem of the text was Nicholas Rowe (1674–1718), who also divided most of the plays into acts and scenes, supplied place-names of the location of each scene, indications of entrances and exits, and a list of dramatis personæ, which are absent from many of the texts in the Quarto and Folio editions. All the acts and scenes in the First Folio *Macbeth* correspond with those in modern editions, however, except that in many modern editions Macduff's encounter with Macbeth at the end of the play makes a separate scene (V. viii). This is quite unimportant on the stage, however. Opposing sides which have hitherto been represented in separate scenes meet together in battle in vii; the 'leafy screens' of the attackers are thrown down in vi and then the enemies meet in vii ending with the two most important. All entrances and exits of characters on the stage of the Folio *Macbeth* correspond with those of modern editions within a few lines, and the text of the play is practically the same as that recognized now.

While knowledge of the text is important for examination study, and, indeed, intelligent textual study can throw much light on an author, it should never be forgotten that the literary and dramatic aspects of the play are more vital. At the same time, study of the text is the basis of all literary and dramatic study.

Outstanding criticism of *Macbeth*

Critical material on *Macbeth* is inexhaustible, and the student may not know where to turn. Here, therefore, is a selection of the most helpful.

Shakespearian Tragedy. A. C. Bradley. Macmillan. Lectures IX and X.

Shakespearian Tragedy. H. B. Charlton. C.U.P. pp.141–88.

Shakespeare. John Masefield. Williams and Norgate. pp.195–202.

Shakespeare: his Mind and Art. Edward Dowden. Kegan Paul. pp.103–4 and Chapter V, Section II. (A conventional study, perhaps not so stimulating, but thoughtful and thorough.)

Shakespeare Criticism. Ed. D. Nichol Smith. Humphrey Milford. pp.143–99, 297–301, 307–17, 346, 372–8.

Textual notes

Act I Scene i

Three witches in thunder and lightning in 'a desert place' agree to meet Macbeth 'upon the heath' 'when the battle's lost and won', and in a moment or two they slink off chanting a riddle.

A scene in a play may do one or more of the following:

1 Advance the action.
2 Create an atmosphere.
3 Develop a character.
4 Give dramatic relief – contrast.
5 Make an impression of the flight of time between two other scenes.

This scene is a scene of atmosphere. It is very important dramatically as setting the atmosphere for the whole play at the very beginning, an atmosphere of mystery, weirdness, horror, superstition and evil. As Coleridge puts it, it strikes 'the key-note of the character of the whole drama'. And these loathsome hags croaking out riddles in a desert place want some traffic with Macbeth. What can it be? There is a sense of something dread hanging over our heads. The suspense of the audience is aroused.

Notice the use of sympathetic background. This is an old device, and is universal, from the greatest literature to the cheapest films, whereby the weather is harmonized with the events in the story, at once intensifying the atmosphere and broadening it, as if not only the two or three people in the story were affected but the whole universe. The strife and turmoil in nature echoes the strife and turmoil in

1 Duncan's kingdom, divided against itself.
2 Macbeth's castle, where king, guest and kinsman is murdered.
3 (Most important of all) Macbeth's mind.

The student would do well to note the amount of *Macbeth* that happens at night-time or in a dark place, and the number of references to darkness. The deeds of Macbeth will not bear the light of day.

For comments on the verse of this scene see p.8.

Three A magic number. Nine (three times three) was a number of particular efficacy. See I. iii. 35–6.

lost and won One side loses and the other wins. Like I. ii, it gives the impression that the witches are talking in riddles.

Graymalkin grey cat.

Paddock toad. The witches' familiar spirits, in the shape of animals, are calling them.

Anon at once. *Lit. in one.*

Act I Scene ii

News straight from the battlefield is brought to Duncan, King of Scotland, telling of 'brave Macbeth's' great victory over rebels aided by a foreign foe. Duncan proclaims Macbeth thane of Cawdor in place of the defeated rebel leader.

This scene gives the situation in Scotland at the period the play opens.

Notice the jerkiness of the Sergeant's speech, as of a man out of breath and in pain, and at the same time eager to get out his message.

The dramatic importance of the scene is that it praises Macbeth's strength and bravery before his appearance. Learn the tributes spoken by the Sergeant, Duncan and Ross. Suspense is aroused. We long for the appearance of such a hero. The opinion the audience has already formed of him makes him seem more impressive when he does appear. After all, the part of Macbeth is taken only by an actor, and 'the best in this kind are but shadows, unless imagination mend them'. Such tributes paid before he appears help the imagination to 'mend' the actor, and the actor to transcend his art. Added to this is a glint of mystery – the witches want dealings with Macbeth – which increases the suspense.

In Shakespeare's early plays the main character appeared on the stage at the outset, e.g. in the History plays. Later on, however, e.g. *Twelfth Night* (1601) onwards, he generally leads up to him in the conversation of minor characters, which is dramatically much more effective. The situation is built up before the main character enters into it. From a practical point of view it also means that the first speech of the main character is not disturbed by the entrance of latecomers: by the time he speaks the audience has 'settled down'.

Another important point in the structure of the play – the higher Macbeth is exalted, the greater his fall.

Duncan might well be grateful to Macbeth, for had it not been for his victory while Duncan was safe behind the lines, Duncan, King of Scotland, would now be a hunted outlaw. Note the ironical fact that but for Duncan's ready acknowledgement of Macbeth's service by making him thane of Cawdor he might never have been encouraged to press on to the crown.

Forres Near the coast, some 25 m. N.E. of Inverness.

of the revolt the newest state the latest news of the revolt.

hardy brave.

choke their art make their skill useless.

Worthy fit.

to that to that end.

western isles Ireland.

kerns and gallowglasses Lightly and heavily armed troops respectively. cf. l. 30, '*skipping* kerns'.

all's too weak Fortune's support of Macdonwald was not sufficient to bring victory, owing to Macbeth's bravery.

which who.

unseam'd him from the nave to the chaps ripped him open from the navel to the jaws.

cousin See I. vii. 13.

As whence . . . break i.e. as storms (discomfort) come from the east (the source of comfort – the herald of day).

surveying vantage seeing his opportunity.

furbish'd burnished, i.e. not yet used.

cracks charges.

memorize make memorable.

Golgotha See *Matthew* XXVII. 33 and *Mark* XV. 22.

I cannot tell i.e. tell what else it was.

thane Corresponding to the English 'earl'.

Fife District between the Firths of Forth and Tay.

cold i.e. with fear. He refers to the scene before the battle – he is starting his story from the beginning.

dismal i.e. it was dismal until Macbeth confronted him.
Bellona Roman goddess of war.
proof tested (*lit. proved*) armour.
Confronted with self-comparisons was a match for him.
Point against point rebellious The point of Macbeth's weapon against the point of that of the rebel (or, strictly speaking, ally of a rebel).
lavish insolent.
composition terms.
Saint Colme's inch Saint Columba's island, Inchcolm, in the Firth of Forth.
dollars The name is derived from the Dutch word 'daler', the name of a sixteenth-century Bohemian coin. There were no dollars in the time of the Macbeth of history. See pp.3–4.
bosom interest cf. *bosom* friendship.
present immediate (the literal meaning).

Act I Scene iii

The three witches are awaiting Macbeth on the heath as he returns from the battle (see Scene i). He comes, accompanied by Banquo; the witches show no interest in Banquo, but hail Macbeth as thane of Glamis (his present title), thane of Cawdor, and 'king hereafter'. When pressed by Banquo to speak to him they say that he shall beget kings, though he be none. Soon afterwards a messenger from the king hails Macbeth as 'thane of Cawdor' (see Scene ii). Macbeth is 'rapt', and the idea of making himself king by disposing of Duncan occurs to him.

The prelude to this scene is full of the trappings of witchcraft.

Macbeth's first words unconsciously echo the last words of the witches in Scene i, and link him at the back of our minds with these evil hags, who surely would not have any dealings with a man unsullied by guilt. It is to meet him that they have come; Banquo just happens to be with him at the time.

Notice the difference between Macbeth and Banquo under the influence of the witches. One is disturbed profoundly, the other takes it in his stride. When Macbeth is 'All hailed' as 'king hereafter', he starts like a guilty thing surprised. Banquo, on the contrary, is level-headed before the witches' prophecies. He sees at once what Macbeth sees only at the end of the play.

Oftentimes, to win us to our harm,
The instruments of darkness tell us truths,
Win us with honest trifles, to betray's
In deepest consequence.

When the witches move to go Macbeth wants to know more, and when they have vanished he wishes that they had stayed. Then one of the prophecies has a swift and startling fulfilment and he is 'rapt'. He cannot get the prophecies out of his mind and twice refers to them in asides to Banquo. All this is very important in deciding whether Macbeth had had any thoughts of murder before he met the witches, and whether for their prey the witches can fasten only upon those who have lent their minds to evil suggestions and thus laid themselves open to their influence.

The witches ignore Banquo, and when he first speaks to them each lays her 'choppy finger' upon her lips. It is only when enjoined to do so by Macbeth that they speak.

swine Illnesses of cattle, especially swine, were popularly attributed to witches in Shakespeare's time.
Aroint thee away with thee.
rump-fed Therefore well-fed.
ronyon scurvy woman.
Tiger A common name for a ship in Elizabethan times.
like a rat without a tail Witches were supposed to be able to take the form of any creature, but it would always be lacking a tail.
do 'carry on', i.e. gnawing the boat, having taken the shape of a rat to do so.
shipman's card compass.
pent-house lid i.e. eyelid. A pent-house is an outhouse.
forbid cursed.
se'n-nights It is curious that we have retained the term 'fortnight' (*fourteen*-night) and yet dropped the corresponding term for a week.
pilot helmsman.
homeward Just at the time when he was most looking forward to reaching land.
posters speedy messengers. cf. *post*-haste (i.e. as speedy as by relays of fresh horses kept at stages along a road).
thine . . . mine Thy side and my side.

foul and fair This is usually taken to refer to the weather, but Macbeth would hardly bother about the weather when he was in the thick of the fight. More likely it refers to the battle – a fierce fight with a happy issue. In Scene i. l. 11 the witches obviously do refer to the weather. Refer to the note at the head of this scene.

call'd reckoned.

choppy chapped.

thane of Cawdor Notice that they greet him as *already* thane of Cawdor and not *to be* thane of Cawdor. This is proof to Macbeth that they have supernatural knowledge, for how else could they have found out the information?

Why do you start? Why does he? Because somebody else knows about his thoughts too!

show appear.

present grace Thane of Cawdor.

great prediction of noble having It is a *prediction* (for he is not thane of Cawdor) and yet you say he *has* the title.

That so that.

beg . . . hate beg your favours nor fear your hate.

Hail! Notice the lesser greeting for Banquo.

get beget.

all hail, Macbeth and Banquo! Although the order of the names is reversed in the next line, in each case the 'all hail' comes next to Macbeth's name.

Stay Evidently the witches make as if to go. Remember that Shakespeare wrote a play to be acted, not read, and much action is apparent from the words of the speakers without stage directions.

Sinel His father.

A prosperous gentleman And Macbeth knew he was a captive rebel! He is trying to find out how much the witches know.

owe have, possess. *Lit. own.*

corporal bodily. (cf. *corporal* punishment.)

insane root root causing insanity. Supposed to be hemlock.

And thane of Cawdor Macbeth always tries to turn Banquo off when he mentions the third 'all hail' – it was what was in his own mind the most.

His wonders . . . or his i.e. he marvels so much that he does not know whether he can find words to praise you.

post messenger. cf. note on 'posters', p.20.

Thy praises in praise of what you did in.
earnest pledge.
why do you . . . robes? Surely it is evident! Macbeth is flustered. Or perhaps he cannot believe his own ears and wants to make sure that it is true.
line strengthen.
vantage See note on 'surveying vantage', p.18.
I know not It is curious, since he had travelled with Ross and their conversation must have turned on what was in everybody's mouth.
Do you not hope . . . to them? He *really* wants to find out what Banquo thinks of the *greatest* prophecy which *lies behind.*
trusted home carried to its logical conclusion.
Win us with honest trifles . . . consequence win our confidence by letting us win small stakes and then betray us on something that really matters. 'A sprat to catch a mackerel.'
Cousins, a word While the audience is listening to Macbeth's soliloquy, Banquo and the others obviously cannot just stand doing nothing. Shakespeare makes them pretend to engage in conversation together. 'Cousins' was used loosely in Elizabethan English; like a man calling a boy 'son' today.
prologues . . . theme Metaphor from the structure of a play.
cannot be good This is what he really feels at the bottom of his heart, but the wish that it may be good is 'father to the thought'.
fears objects of fear.
single May mean 'weak', or 'very'.
state A metaphor – nation.
function . . . not power of action is smothered by surmise, and the only thing real to me is what is not actual (i.e. my being king in the future).
If chance . . . stir if the witches are true prophetesses, what they prophesy will come true whatever I do. Therefore, I may be crowned without taking any step towards it.
strange i.e. new. Metaphor from a new suit.
Time and the hour . . . day It is no use crossing the bridge before we come to it. In rhyme because it has a proverbial ring.
we stay upon your leisure Banquo is politely telling him that they are waiting for him.
Give me your favour excuse me.
wrought agitated. A lie to account for his musings.

your pains . . . to read them I shall never forget the trouble that you have taken. Metaphor from reading a memorandum book.

Act I Scene iv

Duncan receives Macbeth at his palace, warmly thanking him for his services. He further honours him by announcing that he will stay as a guest at his castle.

In the conferring of honours Duncan names his eldest son Malcolm as his heir.

Macbeth goes on in front to let his wife know that Duncan is coming.

Duncan's naming of Malcolm as his heir destroys Macbeth's hope that 'chance may crown' him (Scene iii, l.143).

Macbeth is full of dramatic irony – the difference between the situation as known to the audience and as supposed by the characters of the play or by some of them. Notice the dramatic irony of Duncan's words of Cawdor as he turns to see Macbeth approaching (ll.11–14), and where Duncan says Macbeth's 'care is gone before to bid us welcome' (l.57), whereas really he has spurred on to plot Duncan's murder with his wife.

Contrast Macbeth's forced and fulsome thanks to Duncan with Banquo's brief and sincere acknowledgment.

in commission Commissioned by the king to order the execution.
studied A stage metaphor. To 'study' is the word used of an actor learning his part.
owed See note on 'owe', p.21.
careless The literal meaning of the word – one he had no care for.
more than all can pay than all I can do to repay you – and more. The rhyme gives the effect of clinching it.
safe surely. (cf. *safe and sure*).
begun to plant thee i.e. by bestowing on you the title of thane of Cawdor. Banquo continues the metaphor.
no . . . nor In Elizabethan English a double negative intensifies the idea, instead of logically cancelling it.
seek . . . sorrow He is almost weeping for joy.
estate succession. The throne of Scotland was originally not hereditary, in theory at any rate, though it usually became so in practice, as here.

Prince of Cumberland The title held by the king's 'named' successor (cf. Prince of Wales). Cumberland was originally part of Scotland.

Inverness The site of one of Macbeth's castles (see Scene v).

bind us further to you By becoming our host.

The rest . . . for you The normal word order would be to put 'is labour' at the end of the sentence. – The leisure which is not used in your service is as hard as work.

Stars . . . desires See p.16.

wink at the hand i.e. fail to see what the hand does.

True, worthy Banquo See note on 'Cousins, a word', p.22. Notice that Banquo is not slow to praise his colleague.

Act I Scene v

In her castle Lady Macbeth is reading a letter from Macbeth telling her of the witches' prophecies. She thinks that her husband is too weak-natured to make himself king. Thereupon a messenger comes telling of the king's visit. The news unsettles her for a moment, but she quickly recovers herself, and then she realizes that if she can bring herself to it his visit gives her just the opportunity she wants.

On Macbeth's arrival he greets her lovingly, but she at once refers to the witches' prophecy and goes on to suggest that Duncan must be 'provided for' that very night.

Learn Lady Macbeth's masterly analysis of her husband's character. Incidentally, by this very analysis she lays bare her own character – she would not be or do what she condemns him for. Notice, too, her determination and assurance, 'and *shalt be* what thou art promised'. There is no hesitation and no thought of the consequences. Unlike Macbeth, she never looks beyond the crown.

In her second soliloquy, also well worth learning, she steels herself to the dreadful deed. But the very fact that she needs to repress her more tender feelings is evidence of their existence to begin with. (This is also borne out by Scene vii, ll.54–9 and Act II Scene ii, ll.12–14). The most fitting commentary on this speech is her sleep-walking in Act V. She breaks down under the strain. In the long run Nature sends in the bill.

Her conscience is also shown by her euphemisms. 'He that's

coming must be *provided for*', and 'this night's great *business*'. She cannot look her deed in the face and recognize it for what it is – sheer murder.

Remember that Lady Macbeth has not seen her husband since before he left for battle. Since then he has become Scotland's hero. She gives him no word of pride, pleasure or congratulation; she goes straight to the purpose to which she has just bent every fibre of her being.

Macbeth would rather like to withdraw (apart from his words, he evidently shows it by his expression, see l.60), but is overruled by his wife's stronger personality. So he gives the reply of people who mean 'No' but are too weak to say so, 'Well, I'll think about it' – 'We will speak further'.

With all their faults, Macbeth and Lady Macbeth are fond of each other. The terms in which they address one another are perfectly sincere. Further, Lady Macbeth never dwells on her own pleasure at being queen, it is always Macbeth as king that is before her mind. Shakespeare knew life too well to present melodramatic villains.

report intelligence, knowledge. Their hailing him as thane of Cawdor.

missives messengers, i.e. bearers of missives.

illness should evil tendencies which should.

thou 'ldst have . . . undone you would have a position which can be obtained only by a deed which you fear to do yourself, but if it were done by somebody else you would not wish it undone (so that you could reap the benefit of it).

metaphysical supernatural.

To have thee crown'd already to have crowned you.

Thou 'rt mad to say it The news that Duncan himself is giving her the opportunity she thought she would have to make throws her off her guard for a moment.

is not thy master . . . preparation A subterfuge to account for her slip. She at once regains her self-possession. 'Inform'd for preparation' – sent word so that we might make preparation.

The raven himself is hoarse The idea is suggested by the breathless messenger. The raven was supposed to be a bird of ill omen.

mortal deadly.

remorse pity
nor keep peace . . . it nor intervene between the purpose and its accomplishment (in the reverse order).
sightless invisible.
wait on As ministers *ministering to*. Or the sense may be 'wait for'.
pall wrap as in the black cloak over a coffin. A most apt word here.
peep As if just a peep would be enough to make heaven cry 'Stop!'.
ignorant i.e. of the future.
Shall sun . . . see The short line emphasises her determination.
beguile the time deceive people.
Which shall . . . masterdom What disillusionment lies in store! Notice that she particularly mentions '*nights and* days'. The best commentary on this is III. ii. 17–19.
To alter favour ever is to fear to alter your face (i.e. look down) is always a sign of cowardice.

Act I Scene vi

Lady Macbeth welcomes Duncan to her castle.

Notice

1 The contrast between this restful scene and the scenes before and after it, like a shaft of light between dark clouds.

2 Dramatic irony. (a) Duncan admires the place where he is to meet his doom. (b) The last glimpse we have of him is where he is graciously taking his greatest enemy by the hand. (c) Ll.22–3.

3 Duncan's graciousness and thanks, which enlist the sympathy of the audience for him.

4 The frequency of the words 'host' and 'guest', impressing Lady Macbeth's foul violation of the laws of hospitality.

Hautboys oboes.
approve prove.

his loved mansionry loving it for building its nest.
jutty A part that juts out. The same word as *jetty*.
coign of vantage convenient corner. cf. 'surveying vantage', note p.18.
The love . . . for your trouble The love people show to us (the royal plural) sometimes gives us 'trouble', but we always look at the motive and thank them on account of their love. So I show you how you should pray God to reward us for your pains (on account of our visit)

and thank us for any trouble caused you (for we regard you highly and do you a great honour by coming to your castle). 'Still' = always; ''bid' = pray; ' 'ild' is a corruption of *yield*, i.e. reward.

hermits i.e. we pray for you.

coursed chased.

purveyor harbinger (see Scene iv, l.45). *Lit.* for the arrangement of a supply of food. Now the word has this idea only, without the idea of going ahead.

holp Here the past participle of 'to help'.

compt account.

their audit Metaphor of a steward (*auditor*) rendering his account.

Act I Scene vii

Towards the end of supper Macbeth has slipped away to think over things, and he decides not to murder Duncan. Lady Macbeth follows him and makes him reverse his decision.

Left to himself Macbeth's decision is 'We will proceed no further in this business'. This is quite definite. There is no 'I think' or 'Perhaps' about it.

The motives that bring him to this decision are a curious mixture of good and evil.

1 Fear of the consequences (consequences on earth – he will risk the life to come). (Contrast Lady Macbeth's speech in Scene v, beginning 'The raven himself is hoarse'. Less imaginative, she is untroubled by any thoughts of consequences.)
2 He is Duncan's kinsman, subject and host.
3 Duncan has been a good king.
4 Nothing but ambition incites him.
5 (after Lady Macbeth has come in) Duncan has honoured him, and people think well of him.

Then Lady Macbeth turns him right round to 'I am settled'.

Macbeth. 'We will proceed no further in this business.'
Lady Macbeth. You do not love me. You are a coward.
I am a woman, but I would be more resolute.
Macbeth (wavering). 'If we should fail?'
Lady Macbeth. Here are plans whereby we shall not fail.
Macbeth. In turn, *he* suggests plans.
Finally – 'I AM SETTLED'.

His last speech is quite in his wife's manner, and this emphasises how much he is under the power of her personality. Ll.79–80 echo the speech in Scene v where she sets her teeth to do the deed, and ll.81–2 are even cast in the same language as her

To beguile the time,
Look like the time; bear welcome in your eye,
Your hand, your tongue: look like the innocent flower,
But be the serpent under 't.

Sewer head waiter, whose duty it was to supervise the arrangement of dishes on the table. He comes before the '*divers* Servants' with the dishes.
If it were done . . . quickly if the murder would be done *with* when it was done, then the sooner done the better.
trammel up entangle – as a net, so that there would be no consequences: the consequences would be captured.
his surcease its conclusion, cessation.
bank and shoal of time A lifetime is just a mere island bank in the great ocean of eternity (perhaps suggested by the metaphor of catching in a net).
jump risk.
still always. See note on 'The love . . . for your trouble', pp.26–7.
return to plague the inventor beat the master at his own (evil) game.
faculties official powers.
clear i.e.. of blame or guilt.
taking off Euphemism. The same applies as is said of Lady Macbeth. p.24–5.
like a naked new-born babe The simile suggests compassion for something helpless.
cherubin Plural here. For the idea cf. *Psalm* xviii, 10.
sightless couriers of the air. The winds. For 'sightless' see note p.26.
tears Caused by the deed's being blown 'in every eye'.
drown the wind As with a shower of rain the wind ceases.
I have no spur . . . intents The metaphor is suggested by the previous one, 'horsed upon the sightless couriers of the air', and in turn leads to the one of trying to mount a horse and vaulting too far and coming to grief on the other side.
Was the hope . . . freely? Now we know for sure why Macbeth started when the witches 'all hailed' him as 'king hereafter'. He had

thought of it before. See also ll.47–52. The metaphor is from a man who has slept off his drunkenness but wakes up 'green and pale' from the effects of the night before and does not feel fit to tackle what he had set his mind on. 'Dress'd' continues Macbeth's metaphor.

Letting 'I dare not . . . would' letting your fear control your ambition.

The poor cat i' the adage The cat wanted the fish in the water but did not want to wet her feet.

Prithee, peace Macbeth is stung by her tongue.

is none i.e. loses his manhood by doing evil.

beast In antithesis to Macbeth's 'man'.

break communicate. cf. '*break* the news'.

more than what you were i.e. king.

did then adhere then gave opportunity.

you would make both At that time you would have liked to have made both (i.e. a time and a place for the murder).

I have given suck . . . this See p.24.

We fail? How is this said? It may be in the tone of 'Well then, we fail, and there's an end of it', or '*We* fail! The very idea!'. It is more likely to be the second.

screw your courage to the sticking-place Metaphor from tuning a stringed musical instrument.

convince overcome (Lat. 'vincere', to conquer).

the warder of the brain The brain was supposed to be divided into three sections. Memory formed the outside section, and so was the guardian of the other two. – The chamberlains shall not remember what has happened.

receipt receptacle.

limbech alembic – the cap of a still, through which vapours pass to a receiver. i.e. memory shall pass through the brain without being received by it.

quell murder.

received accepted as true, believed.

bend up Metaphor from straining a bow.

Revision questions on Act I

1 What is the dramatic value of Scene i?

2 What is the audience's idea of Macbeth's character before his appearance on the stage?

3 Show how the witches influence Macbeth and Banquo differently and account for this.
4 What is the effect of the witches' prophecies on Lady Macbeth?
5 What does Lady Macbeth show of her own character in her analysis of her husband's character?
6 Give the story of the plot and your impression of the characters of Macbeth and Lady Macbeth up to the end of Act I.
7 Do you think that Macbeth would have murdered Duncan without (a) the prophecies of the witches, (b) the instigation of his wife?

Act II Scene i

In the middle of the night Banquo hands Macbeth the present of a diamond sent by Duncan to Lady Macbeth just before he went to bed, as an acknowledgment of her hospitality.

Banquo mentions the three witches, but Macbeth puts him off and Banquo goes. Macbeth tells a servant to bid Lady Macbeth 'strike upon the bell' when his drink is ready. No sooner is Macbeth alone than he has a horrid vision of a dagger. When it is gone he determines to get the murder over quickly. The bell rings (it is his signal) and he goes to do the deed.

The conversation between Banquo and Fleance is one of many instances which shows how the scene was brought home naturally, within the play, to an audience without scenery, perhaps watching this midnight scene with the sun shining in their faces (see p.9).

Banquo's further speech gives a sense of restless anxiety. Presentiment is a fundamental principle in Shakespearian drama. It heightens the suspense.

It is not the thought of killing which causes Macbeth's hallucination. 'Bellona's bridegroom', who could unseam a man 'from the nave to the chaps', would know none of this loathing of blood and killing. It is his guilty conscience.

husbandry thrift, economy.
Their candles i.e. the stars. 'Their' refers to 'heaven'.
Take thee that too This would be quite clear on the stage. Banquo would hand him his shield or his dagger.

Give me my sword As he hears an approaching step.

largess to your offices 'tips' to your servants' quarters.

This diamond . . . hostess The last act of Duncan is to make a generous gift to his greatest enemy! (Dramatic irony.) Notice the word 'hostess' again. cf. Act I Scene vi, and see p.26.

shut up gone to bed.

Our will . . . defect our will, therefore, was held in check by our deficiencies, i.e. what we wanted to do was limited by our unpreparedness, owing to the short notice we were given.

when we can . . . time This is the second time that Macbeth has said this (see I. iii. 153–5). He puts it off again.

At your kind'st leisure when you are kind enough to make it convenient.

If you shall cleave . . . make honour for you Does Macbeth mean, 'If, when I become king, you support me, I will honour you', or 'If you will agree to a time when we can have our talk, I shall be only too pleased'? Banquo's reply would seem to indicate the former. Naturally, Macbeth does not want to be specific.

none i.e. no honour.

franchised free (from guilt).

I shall be counsell'd I will listen to what you say.

when my drink is ready A mere fetch.

sensible to feeling as to sight able to be felt as well as seen. 'Sensible' = apparent to the senses.

heat-oppressed feverish.

Mine eyes . . . rest if the dagger is not there my eyes (which see one) are cheated (mocked by the other senses); if the dagger is there, my eyes (which see it when I cannot grasp it) are worth all the other senses.

dudgeon handle.

informs thus takes this *form*.

abuse deceive.

curtain'd Peacefully 'tucked up' ('shut up', l.16). One has only to think of the beds of Shakespeare's time surrounded by curtains.

Hecate Goddess of witchcraft.

wither'd 'Like a ghost' (l.56).

his watch Murder's watch ('watch' in the sense of 'watches of the night').

Tarquin Son of the last of the ancient legendary kings of Rome. His rape of Lucretia was the immediate cause of the expulsion of the Tarquins from Rome. This forms the subject of Shakespeare's poem *Lucrece*.

horror i.e. of silence.

Words The subject. 'Gives' is the verb and 'too cold breath' the object. i.e. the longer we talk about doing a thing the more our enthusiasm for it cools. Macbeth had already found this to be true for himself in talking over the murder of Duncan (Act I Scene vii).

Act II Scene ii

Lady Macbeth is waiting for the return of Macbeth from murdering Duncan. When he comes he is all nerves and has made the mistake of bringing the daggers back with him. He cannot steel himself to take them back, so Lady Macbeth goes with them.

While she is away there is the noise of knocking on the gate. When she returns she grasps the situation at once and hurries Macbeth off to bed.

Notice how the atmosphere of terror is intensified by strange sounds heard or imagined, by the staccato question and answer when Macbeth comes down, by Macbeth's exaggerated imagination, and finally by the knocking on the gate.

Lady Macbeth keeps a clear head in an emergency. She sees that he has bungled the crime and that even were it in the face of discovery he could not take the daggers back, so she does it herself. She endeavours to calm her husband by being as unconcerned as possible.

When the knocking takes them unawares she is equal to the situation. She places it at once at 'the south entry' and gives terse, practical directions. Macbeth would have been discovered had she not hustled him about.

Macbeth's last words show that he regrets the deed as soon as it is done.

The knocking brings us 'down to earth', so to speak. We realize that these awful deeds are not happening in a vague, unreal world, far away, but in 'the world which is the world of all of us'.

The scene is full of dramatic irony in the light of subsequent events. Macbeth *has* murdered his sleep. And he was nearer the mark when he said that all great Neptune's ocean would not wash the blood clear from his hand than Lady Macbeth with her, 'A little water clears us of this deed': to the end he felt 'his secret murders sticking on his hands'. Similarly, Lady Macbeth's 'So, it will make us mad'.

owls And crickets (l.16) were creatures of ill-omen.

grooms servants.

possetts A thick drink made chiefly with ale, milk and eggs.

Confounds ruins.

Had he not resembled . . . done't See p.24.

ravell'd sleave tangled skein. Notice the quick succession of metaphors in these lines.

What do you mean? She, unimaginative, just cannot understand him.

gild . . . guilt. Is it natural that Lady Macbeth should pun at such a moment? At times of great anxiety the mind seeks relief in a trivial occupation. We often read in the newspapers of men trapped and in great pain jesting with their rescuers.

To us there does not seem much resemblance between the colour of gold and that of blood, but the colour red was popularly ascribed to gold in the Middle Ages, e.g. the oft-recurring phrase in the ballads, 'goud red gowd'.

Neptune Roman god of the sea.

incarnadine dye red. (cf. *carnation.*)

Your constancy hath left you unattended your firmness has forsaken you.

poorly with such poor spirit.

To know . . . myself I cannot know myself without knowing the deed I have done, therefore it were best not to know myself (and remain 'lost' in my thoughts).

Act II Scene iii

The people at the gate (Macduff and Lennox) are kept waiting while the porter gets roused. Macduff has come early at the bidding of the king – 'to call timely' on him.

He soon discovers the murder. The alarum-bell rings and the whole household is in commotion. Malcolm and Donalbain, the king's two sons, decide that best safety lies in separate flight.

The Porter's speech is very important dramatically. It offers

1 Relief. The feelings of the audience have been worked up to such a pitch that laughter comes as a welcome relief. If the emotional pitch were not lowered, every one of the audience would be feeling, 'Oh, if only I could laugh!'
2 Contrast, making the tragedy seem more tragic and the comedy more comic.
3 A sense of ordinary life. (See p.32.)
4 An impression of the passing of time, giving Macbeth and Lady Macbeth an opportunity to wash the blood off their hands.
5 Dramatic irony. Macbeth's castle is indeed hell, and a porter to Macbeth a 'devil-porter'.

The Porter's speech is far more than a piece of comedy thrown in. It is bound up with the rest of the play. – The Porter has had ample opportunity to get drunk on the strength of Duncan's 'tips', and several of his remarks are connected with his half-dressed state, for he has only had time to throw on a few clothes.

Here and in Scene iv there is much use of sympathetic background (see p.16) – unparalleled disturbance within and unparalleled disturbance without.

After the discovery of the murder notice the way Macbeth and Lady Macbeth act their parts. Macbeth over-acts. Anyone could see what Macduff means when he says,

> Most sacrilegious murder hath broke ope
> The Lord's anointed temple, and stole thence
> The life o' the building.

Lennox does at once, but Macbeth feigns not to understand. The far-fetched metaphors of Macbeth's description of the body of Duncan and the daggers of the grooms sound forced, betraying the way he is striving for effect. Contrast, too, the language in which Macbeth announces the death of their father to Malcolm and Donalbain with the plain statement of Macduff.

> *Macbeth.* The spring, the head, the fountain of your blood
> Is stopp'd; the very source of it is stopp'd.
> *Macduff.* Your royal father's murdered.

Unreal feeling instinctively tries to disguise itself in words. The more we feel, the less we speak. Macbeth spoke too much.

Lady Macbeth makes a mistake when she is first told of the murder and ejaculates 'What, in our house?' Were she really affected by the death of Duncan the place of his death would be of secondary concern.

Is Lady Macbeth's faint a pretence? If a pretence, it is no doubt to divert attention because she thinks that Macbeth is going too far. But there seems no need to doubt its genuineness. She could contemplate a murder for which she had prepared herself – she had steeled herself to the murder of Duncan in Act I Scene v – but this one takes her unawares and she collapses under the shock.

Everything does not go quite so well as the two criminals planned in I. vii. 74–9. Notice Lennox's 'Those of his chamber, *as it seem'd*, had done't'; and Donalbain's last words obviously show suspicion of Macbeth.

By their flight Malcolm and Donalbain play into Macbeth's hands. They draw suspicion on themselves and leave Macbeth no rival claimant to the throne. From the point of view of personal safety flight was no doubt the wiser course, but it showed that they set personal safety above public duty.

old Intensifies the idea, i.e. plenty of. The Porter, disturbed from his drunken sleep, is grumbling at the amount of work he has to do.

Here's a farmer In some productions of *Macbeth* the drunken Porter, only half dressed, tries to get his arm through the sleeve of his doublet, then, as he holds the doublet at arm's length, he thinks it is another person.

on the expectation of plenty Evidently he had hoarded corn to sell at a high price in lean times, but a good harvest made corn plentiful and cheap, and ruined him. This is thought to allude to the bumper crop of 1606, and, if so, helps to fix the date of the play.

equivocator Henry Garnet, a Jesuit, defended equivocation when on trial for his part in the Gunpowder Plot, March 1606. No doubt there are many topical references in Shakespeare's plays which gave a 'spice' to contemporary audiences but are quite lost on modern audiences.

scales i.e. of Justice.

Stealing out of a French hose Skimping his cloth and so stealing some of the material he had been given to make breeches according to French fashions. This is also a hit at the dominance of French fashions in England.

roast your goose Heat your iron. So called because the handle of a tailor's iron resembled the neck of a goose.

But this place is too cold for hell He is only half dressed.

remember the porter He is not too drunk to ask for a 'tip'! Macduff and Lennox have been kept waiting so long that they bound in without thinking of a gratuity for the porter.

the second cock Three o'clock a.m.

But yet 'tis one Although you are glad to do it, it is nevertheless a trouble.

limited appointed.

lay stayed.

Combustion Used in a figurative sense.

the obscure bird the bird of darkness – the owl again.

parallel . . . fellow Strictly speaking, the use of both these words is redundant.

Tongue . . . name thee For the construction see note on 'beg . . . hate', p.21, and for the double negative note on 'no . . . nor', p.23.

Confusion ruin. cf. 'Confounds', note p.33.

Gorgon Whose head turned to stone all beholders.

doom judgment day.

countenance look on.

O gentle lady . . . speak Dramatic irony.

mortality human life. Macbeth is intending to impress by feigned grief, but really he speaks what turns out to be only too true for himself. (Dramatic irony.)

toys trifles.

renown and grace i.e. Duncan, whose attributes they were. The singular idea thus accounts for the singular verb.

vault The earth vaulted by the sky, with a pun on wine 'vaults'.

badg'd marked.

Wherefore did you so? This question is answered by Lennox, III. vi. 15–16.

golden blood See note on 'gild . . . guilt', p.33.

wasteful laying waste.

breech'd i.e. covered.

argument subject.

auger-hole i.e. a tiny, unsuspected place.

Upon the foot of motion ready to go. The metaphors of Donalbain and Malcolm both mean that they have sorrow, but now is not the time to stop and show it.

when we have . . . hid They have rushed in half-clad, and, like the Porter, are feeling the cold.

question deliberate upon.

undivulg'd pretence hidden aims.

put on manly readiness get dressed – perhaps with the idea of putting on armour as well, so as to be ready for any contingency.

the near . . . bloody the nearer related, the more bloody are people's intentions to us (because they would benefit from the crown by our deaths).

dainty of particular about.

Act II Scene iv

Ross talks, first with an old man and later with Macduff, about the strange and violent happenings in the world.

In the course of conversation Macduff says that Macbeth has already gone to be crowned king.

For the function of this scene (of everyday life, not high tragedy) compare sections **3** and **4**, p.34. The lapse of time here is that between the murder of Duncan and Macbeth's appearance as crowned king. Notice the sympathetic background in the first part of the scene and the irony in Macduff's last speech.

The scene advances the plot by letting us know that Macbeth's coronation is arranged.

act A pun on 'deed' and an 'act' of a play.

the travelling lamp Metaphor for the sun. cf. 'candles', note p.30.

predominance An astrological term.

shame i.e. of deeds done on earth.

darkness The subject of 'does entomb'. 'The face of earth' is the object.

On Tuesday last Such little circumstantial details give the truth of fact to fiction.

towering . . . place Terms of falconry.

mousing Therefore seeking her prey on the ground, in opposition to the 'towering' falcon.

pretend See note on 'undivulg'd pretence', above. Lennox was not alone in wondering what advantage the grooms would get from Duncan's murder.

'Gainst nature still Their conduct is of a piece with all the other unnatural events in the world.

ravin devour ravenously.

Scone The famous stone of Scone (an ancient city situated two miles north of the modern Perth) served for many ages as the seat on which the kings of Scotland were crowned and now forms part of the British coronation chair in Westminster Abbey.

Colme-kill The 'cell' of Columbia, burial-place ('store-house') of the ancient kings of Scotland. 'Saint Colme's inch' is in the Firth of Forth (note p.19).

Fife i.e. his home (see note p.18). Macduff, too, is suspicious, though he considers it safer not to say so to Ross in as many words, and he is going to refuse to grace Macbeth's coronation.

our old robes Metaphor for the old state of things. We still use the word 'sit' of the fit of a suit.

Revision questions on Act II

1 Trace the development of the characters of Macbeth and Lady Macbeth up to (but not including) the murder of Duncan.

2 Show, with quotation, how Lady Macbeth's will bears down that of her husband.

3 What is the dramatic value of (a) the Porter's speech, (b) Scene iv?

4 Comment on the way Macbeth and Lady Macbeth act their parts after the discovery of the murder.

5 Point out two speeches of Macbeth which show his insincerity, and one sincere speech.

6 Mention four important facts that we learn in the last scene of the Act.

Act III Scene i

Macbeth is king in the palace at Forres, and Banquo is suspicious that he has murdered Duncan to get there. He makes some enquiry about Banquo's movements and then arranges with two murderers for him and his son Fleance to be slain as they return to the palace to attend a 'solemn supper' at Macbeth's invitation.

This act opens and closes with growing suspicion of Macbeth, at the beginning by one conscious of the witches' prophecies, at the end by a typical observer of events.

Banquo fears Macbeth played 'most foully for't', yet he does nothing to bring the truth to light. Does he hope that by his letting things take their course the prophecy for his descendants will be made good? At any rate this thought is in his mind (ll.3–10).

His words to Macbeth (ll.15–18) are just as insincere as Macbeth's to Duncan, though, of course, this is not to say that his intentions are similar.

See how very cleverly Macbeth finds out essential information for the commission of the murder, ll.19–24 and 36.

Macbeth's continual references to meeting Banquo at the feast and in the council on the morrow are to allay suspicion when the murder becomes known.

Note the intense dramatic irony of ll.29 and 36.

Macbeth's tribute to Banquo (ll.49–54) is all the more noteworthy coming from an enemy. It should be learnt.

Notice Macbeth's inconsistency in accepting the prophecies of the witches for himself, but thinking that he can alter them for Banquo. If they are unalterable for himself, why should they be alterable for Banquo? 'The wish is father to the thought.' As Hecate says in Scene v,

> You all know security
> Is mortals' chiefest enemy.

This time Macbeth is not going to risk being unnerved, so he hires ruffians to do the deed. But he is the real murderer, just as Lady Macbeth was the real murderer of Duncan, although Macbeth bore the knife.

Through this act can be traced Macbeth's growing remorse (see pp.5–6). It began the moment he had committed his first murder –

> Wake Duncan with thy knocking! I would thou could'st!

Sennet A set of notes (strictly *seven*) on a trumpet.

solemn ceremonious.

the which i.e. Macbeth's commands.

grave and prosperous weighty (Lat. 'gravis') and to our advantage (bringing *prosperity*).

strange invention His own guilt, of course.

to make society . . . alone A polite way of intimating that he wants to be left alone.

we . . . ourself The royal 'we'.

while till. Still so used in the West Riding of Yorkshire.

God be with you *Good-bye* is a contraction.

But to be safely thus Either Macbeth was going to say, 'To be safely thus is *everything*' and breaks off with the thought of the man who keeps him from being 'safely thus', or else 'but' means 'except' and the passage then means, 'To be thus is nothing unless we are safely thus'.

royalty of nature Is Macbeth feeling that Banquo is more fitted for the position of king than he is himself? How much of his fear of Banquo is due to realization of Banquo's superiority?

Genius guardian spirit.

unlineal one not an heir to me (not in my *line*).

filed defiled.

eternal jewel soul.

the common enemy of man the devil.

into the list Metaphor from a tournament.

champion me to the utterance fight against me to the extremity (the 'bitter end'), i.e. death, not just a friendly contest for a prize.

Who's there? In his reverie he forgets for a monent that he has sent for the murderers.

this I made . . . conference Anything that needs explaining is better left undone! In any case, as if the murderers care for his reasons! All they want is their pay (ll.84, 126–7 and Scene iii, l.20). Macbeth's explanation is a sop to his own conscience.

pass'd in probation with spent in proving to.

borne in hand kept in expectation, flattered with false hopes.

the instruments i.e. you were the instruments.

them The 'instruments'.

so gospell'd to so governed by the gospel as to.

catalogue list.

ye go for men Macbeth pretends to misunderstand them. They mean, 'We are men enough not to stand it.' He replies, 'Yes, you are men *of a sort*.

shoughs Shaggy dogs. (Variant of *shock*. cf. *shock*-headed.)

water-rugs Shaggy water-dogs.

clept called.
valued file list giving a classification according to value.
housekeeper watchdog.
addition cf. I. iii. 106.
from the bill apart from the list.
Not i' the worst rank of manhood Macbeth uses the same argument by which Lady Macbeth had prevailed upon *him.*
takes your enemy off Euphemism again. cf. note on 'taking off', p.28.
tugg'd with fortune pulled about in wrestling with fortune.
bloody distance deadly enmity. 'Distance' was a fencing term for the space between the antagonists.
my near'st of life my inmost life; my 'very' life, as we say.
avouch answer for. Let the fact that it was my will be sufficient reason for doing it.
Your spirits shine through you Macbeth cuts them short. He is not concerned with *their* reasons and explanations, though he assumes his are necessary.
the perfect spy o' the time the result of enquiry as to the precise time.
something from some distance away from.
always thought . . . clearness always keeping in mind that I require to be free from suspicion. cf. note on 'clear', p.28.
rubs Metaphor from obstacles on a bowling green.
absence the fate. Euphemisms.
Resolve yourselves apart make up your minds a little way off – the 'within' of l.140.
It is concluded . . . tonight cf. this couplet with that closing Act II Scene i, where Duncan's murder is decided on.

Act III Scene ii

Lady Macbeth tries to cheer up Macbeth. He tells her to remember to praise Banquo at the feast and says that early that night 'there shall be done a deed of dreadful note'.

It certainly looks as if Lady Macbeth's 'few words' to Macbeth were to be the suggestions of the very murder which he independently had decided upon!

A sense of guilt has come between man and wife, and keeps them apart. 'Why do you keep alone?' They who hitherto have esteemed and loved one another well now cannot look one another in the eyes. When they murdered Duncan they dealt the death blow to their own love.

Once one has done a thing, it is easier to do it the second time. He whom Lady Macbeth simply had to push into murder the first time now does it without reliance on her, in fact, he gives her only a bare hint of what he has plotted to do.

Compare ll.4–7, not spoken in Macbeth's hearing, with his words ll.19–22.

Once in crime Macbeth sinks deeper and deeper to cover himself. One almost feels that he envies Duncan – 'After life's fitful fever he sleeps well'. His speech ll.13–26 is a terrible comment on Lady Macbeth's assurance in Act I Scene v that the murder of Duncan would 'to all our nights and days to come give solely sovereign sway and masterdom'. The murder has made him the unhappiest person in the play. As a result of it he eats his meal in fear, and 'sleeps in the affliction of these terrible dreams that shake us nightly', and yet, to escape these tortures he is going to commit another murder! Professor Dowden calls the last line but one of the scene the 'motto' of the play.

Compare the dramatic irony of l.2 with that in the previous scene.

content satisfaction. These lines are rhymed, probably because they are in the nature of proverbial sayings.
using cherishing.
without beyond, lit. 'outside'.
the frame of things disjoint the framework of the universe become disjointed.
both the worlds Heaven and earth.
the affliction . . . nightly See p.32 (the last paragraph of the critical material).
peace . . . peace cf. note on 'gild . . . guilt', p..33
ecstasy frenzy.
Gentle my lord A common Elizabethan inversion as in 'Gracious my lord' (V. v. 30), no doubt originating in a desire to emphasise the gentleness, or graciousness, of the person addressed.
your remembrance the reminder you have given me (l.28).
with eye by your looks. Remember that Macbeth has not told her of his plot to murder Banquo.

flattering streams streams of flattery.
make our faces . . . hearts cf. this metaphor with Lady Macbeth's, 'Look like the innocent flower, but be the serpent under it' (Act I Scene v), and with Macbeth's words closing Act I Scene vii.
copy copyhold. A legal term for the tenure of land. cf. l.49.
There's comfort yet i.e. in what you say.
cloister'd round the cloisters.
shard the horny wing-case of the beetle.
yawning making one feel like yawning.
chuck A touch of Macbeth's old tenderness for her. A corruption of *chick.*
seeling blinding. A term from falconry. A hawk's eyes were 'seeled' until he was broken in, by passing a fine thread through his eyelids.
bond The bond under which Banquo and Fleance hold their life.

Act III Scene iii

Banquo is murdered, but Fleance escapes.

Macbeth is getting to trust no one. He sends a third murderer to see that the first two do their job.

His reliance on the witches is such that he has promised a greater reward for Fleance's murder than for Banquo's (l.21).

Why do these ruffians speak in verse? Does the beautiful description of the fading day (l.5) seem appropriate in the mouth of such a character?

He needs not our mistrust we need not mistrust him (the Third Murderer).
offices 'what we have to do'.
To the direction just exactly according to our directions.
subject We should say 'object'.
the note of expectation the list of expected guests.
about round about, a long way round. This, of course, keeps the horses off the stage.
the way the proper thing to do.
affair The reward.

Act III Scene iv

At the beginning of the feast Macbeth slips away to the door and hears from one of the murderers the news of Banquo's murder and Fleance's escape. On his return to the table the company is disturbed by his distraction as he sees the ghost of Banquo. Lady Macbeth makes excuses about his health, until she can pretend no longer, and then brings the function to an abrupt close.

When the guests have gone Macbeth mentions to his wife that he has heard through his spies that 'Macduff denies his person at our great bidding', and that he is going to send to him to make certain.

Lady Macbeth is most resourceful in handling her husband when he sees the ghost and is on the verge of giving herself away. First, she tries a taunt which had succeeded before (ll.58 and 73) That failing, she addresses him in an ordinary matter-of-fact tone, which, we are told, is often effective in calming disordered minds. For the time being this succeeds in restoring him to something like composure.

She keeps the banquet going as long as she can, in the hope that Macbeth will calm down, but as soon as Ross asks a dangerous question (l.116) she interrupts before Macbeth can answer it and breaks up the gathering at once.

When they are alone Lady Macbeth might well have upbraided Macbeth with having given them away. Instead she is only solicitous for his health (l.141). Her unwavering love of him is one of the best points in her character.

Only just recovered from his frenzy, Macbeth contemplates yet another murder (l.128). He lives in a paroxism of fear (ll.131–2, 134–5) and is getting desperate (ll.136–8).

Notice the dramatic irony of l.91 ('Would he were here!').

degrees ranks.
at first and last once for all; or perhaps, from the beginning to the end.
keeps her state remains in her chair of state.
in best time cf. 'in good time'.
require her welcome ask for her welcome to you.
be large be unrestrained, unbend.
dispatch'd Euphemism. cf. 'safe', l.25.
nonpareil unequalled.
whole solid.

casing surrounding, lit. *en*casing.
trenched cut deep. *Trencher* is still the word for a bread-board in some districts.
worm serpent.
ourselves i.e. alone.
cheer welcome, *good* cheer.
the feast . . . welcome the feast which is given without frequent assurances of welcome during its course might as well be bought and paid for.
to feed i.e. *merely* to feed.
From thence . . . ceremony away from home it is ceremony which makes a meal appetising.
remembrancer cf. Scene ii, l.30, and note on 'your remembrance', p.42.
honour roof'd honourable men under one roof.
graced gracious.
challenge accuse.
Thou canst not say I did it Yet it is truer to say he was the murderer of Banquo than that he was the murderer of Duncan.
extend his passion prolong his fit.
Are you a man? Spoken to Macbeth, of course. This is the taunt which had been successful before (I. vii. 49–51).
O proper stuff! Lady Macbeth continues her sarcasm.
flaws gusts (lit. of wind).
to compared with.
Authoriz'd by given on the authority of.
monuments tombs.
Fie, for shame! Lady Macbeth has presence of mind enough not to say, 'Saw whom?'.
purged the gentle weal purged the commonwealth and thus made it gentle. cf. I. vi. 3.
twenty An echo of the murderer's words, l.27.
lack miss.
all to all i.e., all good healths to everybody.
speculation sight.
What man dare, I dare Is Lady Macbeth's taunt still rankling?
arm'd Evidently thinking of the horn on its nose.
Hyrcan Hyrcania was a district S. and S.E. of the Caspian Sea.
nerves sinews.

inhabit have within me.

protest me the baby of a girl say that I am a doll.

I am a man again cf. l.99.

admired remarkable. Therefore, not sarcasm.

overcome The literal meaning, *come over*.

like a summer's cloud i.e. for a short time only.

You make . . . owe you make me a stranger even to my own nature (i.e. I do not know myself). He had thought previously that his own courage was equal to his wife's, now he finds it is not so.

order The 'degrees' of l.1. (We still have the phase 'to *stand on* ceremony'.)

Stones i.e. grave-stones.

augures and understood relations divinations and understanding of the causes of things.

How say'st thou what do you say to it?

denies refuses.

the way i.e. a round-about way.

There's not a one . . . fee'd Typical of the man who had sent a third murderer to keep the first two under observation.

causes considerations.

Strange things The murder of Macduff. When Macbeth is faced with opposition now, the first thought that enters his head is murder.

Which must be acted . . . scann'd Contemplation of them might prevent their being done. This is a thought continually with Macbeth (cf. II. i. 61).

season seasoning.

self-abuse self-deception.

initiate of a beginner, i.e. of one unhardened.

wants lacks.

in deed A euphemism.

Act III Scene v

Hecate, goddess of witchcraft (as in note p.31), grumbles at the witches and tells them to meet her in the morning, for Macbeth will come to consult them.

For comments on the verse of this scene see p.8.

close secret. Still so used.

Acheron An appropriate name for a murky pool near Macbeth's castle, since Acheron was a river of the underworld in classical mythology.
profound deep and therefore ready to fall.
sleights artifices.
artificial produced by art.
confusion ruin, as in note p.36.
He shall spurn fate cf. Scene i, ll.72–3.
security a sense of *false* security.
little spirit attendant spirit.

Act III Scene vi

Lennox talks to another lord of his growing suspicion of Macbeth and is in turn informed of steps being taken for the 'tyrant's' overthrow.

Macbeth has reached the height of his material power. From now on his fortunes steadily decline in face of mounting opposition.

The height of Macbeth's *character* was at his first appearance, and it deteriorates from that very moment.

In Scene iv we see how Macbeth's own better nature is against him; in Scene v how the supernatural forces on which he is relying are against him, and now how the nation he rules is against him.

The tone of Lennox's speech is, of course, ironical. He is sounding the lord, without speaking too openly. Even in this short scene there is an impression of swiftly growing opposition: after Lennox's cautious speech the lord at once speaks openly of 'this tyrant', whereupon Lennox throws off his reserve and follows in the same vein. We are told of the result of Macbeth's summons to Macduff, on which he decided in Scene iv, l.130. We feel that Macbeth's downfall can be only a matter of time. His evil deeds are recoiling upon himself, just as he said evil deeds did, I. vii. 10–12.

Who cannot want who can be without? As in note on 'wants', p.46.
marry An oath by the Virgin Mary, but in effect no stronger than 'indeed'.

gracious cf. l.3; *graced*, Scene iv. l.41; and *grace* in Act II Scene iii (in a speech of Macbeth).
fact deed.
an if.
they should find . . . father i.e. they have not done it yet.
from broad words on account of plain speaking.
'cause he fail'd . . . feast See Scene iv, l.128. Macduff also refused to attend Macbeth's coronation, see II. iv. 35–6.
the most pious Edward Edward the Confessor.
his high respect i.e. the high respect people pay to him.
upon his aid for the purpose of aiding him (Duncan's son).
Free from . . . knives Had he seen the murderer at the banquet?
cloudy i.e. frowning.
distance i.e. from Macbeth.
suffering The normal order would be to place this word after 'country'.

Revision questions on Act III

1 How far do you think Banquo blameworthy in keeping his suspicion of Macbeth to himself?
2 How does Macbeth find out Banquo's movements on the night of the banquet without arousing his suspicion?
3 From Macbeth's soliloquy in Scene i give four reasons why his 'fears in Banquo stick deep'.
4 Why did not Macbeth take his wife into his confidence with regard to the murder of Banquo?
5 Comment on Lady Macbeth's handling of the situation at the banquet.
6 Mention any three of Macbeth's speeches at the banquet which would show to any average intelligence that he feels guilty of some dreadful crime.
7 Compare the last scene of the act with the last scene of Act II. State four important facts that we are told in it.

Act IV Scene i

Macbeth goes to the witches and meets them in a cavern. They tell him (i) to beware the thane of Fife (Macduff), (ii) that 'none of woman born shall harm Macbeth', (iii) that

> Macbeth shall never vanquish'd be until
> Great Birnam wood to high Dunsinane hill
> Shall come against him,

and show him an apparition signifying that the heirs of Banquo shall be kings.

Macbeth hears from Lennox that news has just come that 'Macduff is fled to England', and he determines to take revenge on his wife and children 'and all unfortunate souls that trace him in his line'.

The first part of this scene is masterly in its creation of a loathesome, gruesome atmosphere. Compare what is said of the trappings of witchcraft in Act I Scene i, p.16.

The witches no longer need to go out to seek Macbeth: he seeks them. The first time he met them he wondered whether they were good or evil (I. iv. 130–1), now he has no doubt that they are evil (III. iv. 135 and this scene l.48).

Notice how he 'welcomes' those to whom he has come seeking help (l.48)! He is promised security for himself, but he is burning to know if Banquo's issue shall 'ever reign in this kingdom'. The witches have said they shall once before: what Macbeth wants is not knowledge; he wants them to unsay this part of their prophecy. 'Why do you show me this?' he says, yet he had *demanded* to be shown (ll.104–5), and blames them because their prophecy does not suit him. The irony of it when he exclaims, 'Damn'd all those that trust them!'

The scene closes with his hideous resolution on hearing that Macduff has thwarted him by fleeing to England. As on the first occasion (I. iii. 105) the accuracy of one of the witches' prophecies is again indicated no sooner than it has been uttered, thus strengthening Macbeth's trust in the other prophecies.

hedge-pig hedge-hog.

Harpier Meant to be the name of a demon.

venom The toad was thought to be venomous, like the newt (l.14) and the blind-worm or slow-worm (l.16).

fenny And therefore slimy.

fork forked tongue.

howlet owlet.

gulf gullet.

ravin'd ravenous. cf. note p.38.

yew Associated with death and poisonous to cattle.

sliver'd stripped off down the bark, not a clean break.

eclipse A time of bad omen.

slab slimy.

chaudron entrails.

By the pricking . . . comes Similar to the superstition that burning ears betoken that one is the subject of a conversation near at hand.

yesty foamy.

navigation ships.

bladed in the blade.

lodg'd laid flat.

germens seeds.

sicken be surfeited.

an armed Head Representing Macbeth's, cut off by Macduff.

Thou hast harp'd . . . aright what you have said harmonises with my own fears.

a bloody Child Representing Macduff.

three ears Referring to the threefold salutation.

take a bond of fate make fate sign a bond, so that it will be bound to its agreement. cf. III. ii. 49.

sleep . . . thunder See III. ii. 17–19, and p.32.

a Child crowned . . . hand Representing Malcolm. See V. iv. 4.

the round and top of sovereignty the crown.

Birnam . . . hill Birnam wood is 10 m. or so N.E. of Perth (it was formerly a royal forest), and Dunsinane hill is some 6 m. N. of Perth. The distance between the two is nearly 10 m.

impress conscript (*press* into service).

bodements prophecies.

lease of nature Another legal metaphor. cf. note on 'take a bond of fate', above and on 'copy', p.43.

noise i.e. music.

start i.e. out of the sockets.

the crack of doom the peal of doomsday. cf. 'cracks' referring to cannon-fire, p.18.

glass mirror.

Twofold balls and treble sceptres A compliment to James I, alluding to his double coronation, first at Scone as King of Scotland, and then at Westminster, and to his being the first king over England

Wales and Scotland ('treble sceptres'). The sceptre and the globe form part of the monarch's insignia, as in any portrait of a king in his robes of office.

bolter'd matted. It is significant that this is the memory of Banquo uppermost in his mind. See III. iv. 50–51.

smiles Probably in satisfaction at the knowledge that Macbeth is doomed and that after all his own children shall be kings.

welcome Refer to his *welcome,* l.48.

flighty fleeting. For the thought of this passage cf. III. iv. 139–40.

trace follow.

sights i.e. the witches' apparitions.

Act IV Scene ii

Ross has just told Lady Macduff, who is with her little son, of the flight of her husband. It puzzles her. Then a messenger comes in haste, telling her to escape. But it is too late – murderers break in and kill the boy and pursue Lady Macduff.

This is the most revolting of the murders. The others had a purpose in them – though an evil one, but this is the result of sheer spite, simply because Macbeth was now unable to reach Macduff. Any admiration we may have had for him, still lingering from Act I, is now for ever dispelled.

Macbeth has sunk deeper and deeper into the pit he has dug for himself – his hand has 'subdued itself to what it works in'. He had to be goaded into the murder of Duncan: he decided on the murder of Banquo on his own account, gave Lady Macbeth the hint, and she concurred: this murder he planned without reference to any one (Scene i, ll.144–55). He had an hallucination (the result of a guilty conscience) *before* the murder of Duncan – the mere idea gave it him (therefore he never risked a murder by his own hands again); *after* the murder of Banquo – it took the accomplishment of the deed to bring it; *not at all* for this murder.

The child's prattle before the murder gives a pathetic impression of helplessness and innocence which gains our sympathy for the child and makes the murder appear all the more brutal. Lady Macduff's sense of loneliness when she hears of her husband's desertion of her has exactly the same effect. She is left to her fate without anybody to rely upon, and we feel the more pity for her.

One must judge whether a young child, as the son is evidently meant to be, would have the intelligence to speak so wittily. With regard to Macduff's flight, see what is said of that of Malcolm and Donalbain, p.35. It must be allowed, however, that Macduff would think a journey to get English support the best way of causing Macbeth's downfall, and would never give it a thought that Macbeth could be such a savage as he turns out to be in this scene.

traitors i.e. to our family.
titles claims to property, or the property itself.
coz lit. '*cousin*', but used broadly in Elizabethan English. cf. note p.22.
The fits o' the season the uncertainties of the time.
I dare not speak much further Macbeth had spies everywhere – see III. iv. 131–2.
when we are traitors . . . ourselves when we are counted traitors (by the people) and yet are not conscious ourselves of being traitors. Macduff is reckoned a traitor by his wife, but no doubt he himself thought that he acted rightly.
when we hold . . . fear when we believe rumours owing to our fears. (For 'from' in this sense cf. note on 'from broad words', p.48.)
Each way and move in every direction and with every movement.
It would be my disgrace i.e. I should give way to unmanly weeping.
Sirrah Used playfully. Usually an address to inferiors, or else indicative of contempt.
lime bird-lime.
pitfall pit to catch animals.
Poor The emphatic word. i.e. it is *rich* birds that are 'set for', therefore I need not fear.
swears and lies swears an oath and then breaks it.
in your state . . . perfect I am perfectly aware of your noble rank.
doubt fear, suspect.
homely plain, humble.
To do worse i.e. to leave you unwarned.
shag-ear'd with hairy ears. Some texts read 'shag-hair'd', i.e. rough-haired.

fry a small fish just out of the spawn – carrying on the metaphor from 'egg'.

Act IV Scene iii

Macduff has fled to join Malcolm in England. Malcolm tests his good faith and then accepts him.

Ross soon arrives, bringing news of the murder of Macduff's wife and children. Macduff is unable to grasp it at first, but when he does so he thirsts for revenge. Malcolm decides that now is the time to set off with the forces provided by the king of England.

Successful rebellion needs months of organization, and this long scene gives the effect of prolonged preparation, in contrast with the short scenes of Act V, with their effect of the stir and bustle of a battlefield. Macbeth is still firmly entrenched, and hasty action would bring disaster.

Malcolm tries to find out whether Macduff is genuine by observing his reactions, first of all when his personal honour is suspected and then when his patriotism is put to a subtle test.

There is piercing dramatic irony in the first part of the scene owing to the speakers' ignorance of the murder of Macduff's wife and children, e.g. ll.4–5 and 14.

Notice the way Ross tries to break the news gently. When it is realized, Macduff is stunned at first – he cannot grasp it: three times he asks if it is really true (ll.206, 208 and 211–14).

Macduff just cannot be bothered with Malcom's well-meaning attempts at consolation. Malcolm cannot know such grief – 'He has no children', and there is an end of it. When grief like this comes home to a man, philosophy is vain. Contrast Macduff's real grief, finding expression in dazed outbursts (e.g. ll.211–14) and Macbeth's feigned grief in Act II Scene iii. The more we feel, the less we can speak, usually. It is in situations like this that Shakespeare is so great. Here is real human feeling, not melodrama.

Not until l.227, when Macduff's dazed grief is clearing, does the thought of revenge come to him.

Like syllable a similar cry.
sole mere.

something . . . through me you may get a reward from him on my account (i.e. by ensnaring me).

recoil in an imperial charge turn aside from goodness and virtue in the execution of a royal commission.

hopes Because they depended upon his being received and trusted by Malcolm, so that he could join with him in leading an army to Scotland.

Perchance . . . doubts perhaps even owing to that very action which made me suspicious of you.

rawness reckless haste.

motives influences on one's actions.

Let not . . . safeties i.e. I am not out to dishonour you in my suspicions but to protect myself.

wear thou Addressing tyranny.

affeer'd confirmed.

England i.e. the king of England.

What i.e. what sort of a man.

open'd Like buds, continuing the metaphor in 'grafted'.

confineless harms boundless vices.

Luxurious licentious.

Sudden short-tempered, or violent.

continent restraining (lit, containing).

Convey indulge.

ill-composed affection disposition composed of evil qualities.

sticks deeper cf. III. i. 50.

summer-seeming i.e. short-lived (and therefore not deeply rooted, in contrast with 'avarice').

sword i.e. cause of taking up arms.

foisons plenty.

mere very. Referring to his property as king.

portable endurable.

relish flavour.

the division of each several crime the different manifestations of each separate crime.

untitled usurping, a king without real title to the throne.

bloody-scepter'd Refers to 'nation'.

breed parentage.

Died i.e. lived as if about to die.

passion grief. cf. note on 'extend his passion', p.45.

trains artifices, lures.
modest wisdom plucks me cautious wisdom holds me back.
my first false . . . myself the first time I spoke falsely was this false speaking about myself.
at a point prepared for any emergency.
like our warranted quarrel equal to the justice of our cause.
king Historically Edward the Confessor, but really the passage is another compliment to James I. cf. Scene i, ll.120–1, and notes on 'Twofold balls' and 'treble sceptres', p.50.
stay his cure wait to be cured by him.
convinces overcomes, as in note p.29.
great assay of art utmost efforts of medical skill.
presently immediately, as in note on 'present', p.19.
the evil Scrofula. It was not until 1712 that English monarchs gave up 'touching' to cure 'the evil'. The practice perhaps lasted so long because cures did result after people had been 'touched'. In addition to the king's 'touch' the diseased person received some good advice: firstly, to wash his skin; secondly, to go home and open the window to let the devil out. Personal hygiene was not of a high order in the early seventeenth century, and windows were bolted and every crack stuffed. The man who had been 'touched' had a clean skin, for the first time for months, probably, and the open window that let the devil out let the fresh air in!
here-remain cf. 'here-approach', l.128.
moves solicits.
strangely-visited victims of strange diseases.
mere absolute, as in note on previous page.
stamp coin.
the healing benediction the blessed power of healing.
virtue power.
speak him give him out to be.
My countryman He can tell from his dress.
once The force is '*even* once'.
mark'd noticed. Because they are so common.
modern ecstasy ordinary, common disturbance. 'Ecstasy' as on p.42.
flowers in their caps Perhaps referring to the sprigs of heather in a Highlander's bonnet.
relation too nice report only too precise.

That of an hour's . . . speaker Because by the end of an hour it is stale news – many other crimes have been committed since then.
they were well . . . 'em Distinguish between this verbal irony and dramatic irony. Ross is quite aware of the double meaning in his words.
out i.e. in rebellion.
witness'd made credible.
power army, forces.
gives The subject is 'Christendom'.
latch catch.
fee-grief grief of a single person.
quarry i.e. bodies. A metaphor from hunting – the murdered game.
Dispute fight against.
naught worthless. A much stronger word than the present-day *naughty*.
Convert change.
if he scape, heaven forgive him too if he escape my sword, it shows I am as bad as he, and therefore Heaven forgive us both. Or it may mean, 'Heaven forgive me as well, for letting him escape.'
Our lack . . . leave nothing more remains to be done but to take our leave.
Is ripe for shaking Metaphor from shaking ripe fruit off a tree.
Put on instigate, incite.
their instruments i.e. themselves.

Revision questions on Act IV

1 Contrast the verse spoken by the witches and that spoken by the human characters.
2 State the prophecies of the witches in Scene i. What is their effect on Macbeth?
3 What do you think of Macduff's action in leaving his wife and children?
4 Is Malcom's suspicion of Macduff justifiable?
5 Describe (a) the way in which Ross unburdens his news to Macduff, (b) the effect the news has upon Macduff.

Act V Scene i

A doctor, called by one of the waiting-gentlewomen, sees Lady Macbeth walk in her sleep and hears her utter her guilty secrets.
In connection with this scene p.24 should be re-read.

Psychologists tell us that anything repressed in waking life tends to recur (usually in a symbolic form) in dreams. Nature gets her own back when the conscious mind is not on the alert. This shows Shakespeare's truth to life. He knew nothing of psychology *as such*, but this is exactly what happens in the case of Lady Macbeth. She had repressed not only all mention of dangerous secrets but of set purpose she had repressed her own womanly nature (Act I Scene v). The intense emotional disturbances she has been through as a result have exhausted her nervous energy, and nature tries to set the balance right by letting the repressions find their release in her sleep, when she is powerless to prevent it.

The student will readily trace the various memories which escape her. In addition, for the first time we know that, in spite of all her brave words, Lady Macbeth was not unafraid of the world to come – 'Hell is murky!'.

Incidentally, judging from the next scene (ll.13 and 23) Macbeth is not far from madness, though it must be remembered that these are comments of his enemies.

Dunsinane See note on 'Birnam . . . hill', p.50. Macbeth's castle was situated on Dunsinane hill.

take forth paper . . . seal it A recollection of Macbeth's letter.

effects of watching actions of waking life.

close hidden.

she has light . . . command She who had invoked the aid of darkness – 'Come, thick night' (Act I Scene v) – is now afraid of the dark!

washing her hands This and much of what follows is reminiscent of the situation immediately following the murder of Duncan.

a quarter of an hour A realistic touch of circumstantial detail. cf. note on 'On Tuesday last', p.37.

afeard? A taunt she had found effective with Macbeth more than once.

will these hands ne'er be clean? The bitter reality, contrasted with her casual, 'A little water clears us of this deed' (II. ii. 67).

this starting A recollection of the banquet scene.

go to An expression of mild reproof.

all the perfumes of Arabia cf. Macbeth's 'all great Neptune's ocean' (II. ii. 60).

what's done cannot be undone Practically her very words, III. ii. 12.

annoyance harm. He is thinking (with justification, as it turns out) that she may try to commit suicide.

mated paralyzed, numbed. cf. 'check-*mated*' in chess.

Act V Scene ii

The dissentient Scottish lords are about to join with the English forces (under Malcolm and Macduff) near Birnam Wood. We learn that Macbeth finds difficulty in controlling his men.

For the effect of these short scenes see p.53. The impression of rush and hurry is all the more marked as the successive scenes take us alternately to each set of combatants.

power army, as in note p.56.

dear touching them very closely. The word intensifies the meaning whether good or bad: in Shakespeare's time one could have a *dear* friend or a *dear* enemy.

alarm call to arms.

the mortified man The hermit who has lived a life of mortification of the flesh and stifling of earthly passions like revenge.

Who knows . . . brother The uncertainty of Caithness adds a touch of reality. Life is full of such uncertainties.

unrough i.e. beardless.

Protest are out to show. cf. note on 'protest me the baby of a girl', p.46.

their first of manhood their manhood for the first time.

buckle his distemper'd cause control his disorganized party. A natural metaphor for one who has just girded himself for battle.

Now does . . . hands See p.32–3.

minutely . . . faith-breach every minute revolts reproach his breach of faith.

pester'd troubled, perplexed.

to recoil for recoiling.

medicine May perhaps mean 'doctor'. But, in any case, Malcolm is meant.

of the sickly weal for the sickly commonwealth. cf. note on 'purged the gentle weal', p.45.

pour we . . . of us to purge our country let us shed every drop of our blood.

the sovereign flower Again, probably, Malcolm is meant. Such a change of metaphor is characteristic of Shakespeare's later style.

Act V Scene iii

In his castle Macbeth hears of the advance of the English force and in his desperation, in spite of his better judgment, still puts his faith in the witches' prophecies. He determines, whatever happens, to fight to the end.

Macbeth has been driven to retreat to his castle and prepare for a siege. His bitterness is increased by realization of the motive from which people serve him, ll.27–8.

The bravado of ll.9–10 agrees little with the tone of sick despair of his other words in the scene, especially ll.22–8.

His state of mind can be judged from ll.48–58. First of all he tells an attendant to put his armour on, then to pull it off, then to bring it after him. No wonder 'Some say he's mad' (Scene ii, l.13).

Not until l.37 does he enquire after his former 'dearest love', 'dearest partner of greatness', though the Doctor has been there all the time.

Contrast the disaffection of Macbeth's followers and the loyalty of Malcolm's. Contrast too the loyalty of the Sergeant in Macbeth's army in Act I Scene ii with the lack of interest of his followers now.

Is there a touch of irony in Macbeth's calling for Seyton (*Satan*)?

them The thanes referred to in l.7, the lords appearing in the previous scene.

taint be infected.

English epicures The accusation of luxurious living was a common one brought by the Scots against the English, as meanness was by the English against the Scots. The Scots came from a poorer country.

sway am directed.

over-red i.e. with blood.

lily-liver'd cowardly. The liver was supposed to be the seat of courage.

patch fool. The professional clown wore motley, or *patched* clothes (made up of pieces of many colours).

push attack.

cheer . . . way 'Chair' and 'may' are suggestions for emendation giving striking antitheses.

skirr scour, the word used in 1.56.

thou In Shakespeare's time the usual (though not absolutely constant) form of the pronoun in addressing one of inferior rank, 'you' being the form between equals or to superiors, as when Seyton asks Macbeth, 'What is your gracious pleasure?'.

oblivious *causing* forgetfulness.

staff lance.

dispatch hurry up. Spoken to the attendant who is putting on his armour.

Act V Scene iv

The two armies against Macbeth have combined forces (as forecast in Scene ii). Malcolm gives orders that every soldier shall 'hew him down a bough and bear 't before him' to screen their numbers.

Contrast the confidence of Malcolm, comparatively inexperienced in arms, and the more cautious optimism of Macduff and Siward, old campaigners, who realize that a battle is not won till it is over, and, while hoping for the best, are prepared for the worst.

discovery spies. Abstract for concrete.

setting down i.e. to begin a siege.

given gained, given *to* them.

more and less great and small.

our just censures . . . event our right judgments wait for the actual result (of the battle), i.e. do not let us be over-confident – 'count our chickens before they are hatched'.

decision certainty.

owe Evidently used here in the modern sense.

Thoughts speculative . . . arbitrate speculations tell only of uncertain hopes, but fighting must decide the actual result. 'Strokes' is the subject of 'must arbitrate', and 'certain issue' the object.

Act V Scene v

Macbeth decides to gather his 'strength' within his castle and 'laugh a siege to scorn'.

Then comes news (1) that Lady Macbeth is dead, (2) that Birnam Wood is moving. Thereupon Macbeth cancels his previous order for 'Arm, and out!'. He will at least die fighting, he says.

When Macbeth hears of the death of her who aforetime was 'his dearest love', his 'dearest partner of greatness', his only comment is that he cannot be bothered with it now and that it is a pity she could not have waited a bit. After the first crime they had kept apart – 'Why do you keep alone?' – now it has come to this. How would it have affected him had he been told the news on his return from the battle against the rebels? All his sensibilities have been blunted.

For philosophy which is the result of a wasted life, see ll.24–8. The life which was to have 'solely sovereign sway and masterdom' is brought to this pitch by guilt. Contrast this speech with the philosophy of many a man who has made something of his life.

Notice Macbeth's reactions to the news that Birnam Wood appears to be moving (l.35). He *knows* that the Messenger is no liar: he knows that in some way it *must* be true. The heat of his outburst is a measure of his fear of believing it.

forc'd reinforced.
fell of hair scalp. 'Fell' = skin. cf. *fell*monger.
treatise story.
Direness horrors.
once *even* once, as in note p.55.
Life's but . . . more Another stage metaphor. cf. I. iii. 128–9. II. iv. 5–6. 'Struts and frets', i.e. in pride or annoyance, referring to his changing part.
a tale . . . fury Continuing the stage metaphor – a ranting actor.
Gracious my lord cf. note on 'Gentle my lord', p.42.
cling shrivel up.
pull in rein in, check.
harness armour.

Act V Scene vi
Before Macbeth's castle Malcolm tells his troops to throw down their 'leavy screens' and gives battle-orders to his commanders.

show appear, as in note p.21.
battle battalion.

we The royal 'we'. This is itself shows his confidence of success. Similarly, note how he takes upon himself his position as king and gives instructions to Siward and Macduff as if he had been doing it all his life.

Act V Scene vii

In the battle Macbeth slays young Siward. Elsewhere success is with the attackers, and we hear that Macbeth's castle is 'gently render'd'.

What better metaphor could there be to express the spirit of desperation in which Macbeth meets his end than, 'They have tied me to a stake'? He knows that the end will be only a matter of time, but he will sell his life as dearly as possible.

When two of the prophecies have failed, any ordinary person would say, 'Well, the chances are that the other will fail too'. Yet although he certainly does begin 'To doubt the equivocation of the fiend, that lies like truth' (Scene v, ll.43–4), having lost twice Macbeth stakes all on a third throw, in spite of everything putting his trust in the third prophecy, hoping against hope.

A sense of his remaining power is given by his killing young Siward. This gives the impression now that to conquer him will not be easy, and makes the victory over him later seem a greater one.

bear-like Bear-baiting was a popular Elizabethan sport.
course The technical term for the dogs' attack on the bear.
kerns boors, not regular troops. A contemptuous use, not as in 'kerns and gallowglasses', note p.18.
staves lances, as in note p.60.
bruited announced by noise.
itself professes 'Itself' is the object of 'professes'.
strike beside us This may mean that they deliberately avoided hitting us by aiming beside us, or that they have come over to our side and fought with us.

Act V Scene viii

In another part of the battlefield Macduff meets Macbeth, who still thinks that he is invulnerable by the witches' prophecy. But he is unnerved when Macduff tells him that he was not 'born', but was 'from his mother's womb untimely ripp'd', and he is slain (off the stage) and his head is exhibited. Malcolm is hailed as king by his thanes, and he makes them Scotland's first earls.

Lines 5–6 come as rather a surprise at this stage of Macbeth's career. He is not quite an animal.

It has taken Macbeth all this time to see what Banquo saw at once. cf. ll.19–22 with I. iii. 123–6.

At the end fear of public derision – 'to be baited with the rabble's curse' – outweighs Macbeth's fear of 'the life to come', and so he dies fighting. In his despair and world-weariness lies the tragedy, not in his death.

It is intense dramatic irony that l.36 should be put into the mouth of Siward. He says that you cannot expect to win a battle without losing *some* men, unaware that his own son is one of the killed. It is easy to talk of death in general terms: little does he know how soon it is to be brought home to him.

Compare the effect of sudden grief on Siward and on Macduff (see p.53). At first neither can grasp it. Siward here says, 'Then he is dead?'. This is true to life. Again, true grief says little.

Is it not a supreme stroke of dramatic irony that in announcing the death of Lady Macbeth Malcolm uses the same euphemism Macbeth had used for the murder of both Duncan and Banquo – '*Took off* her life' (l.71)?

Like most of Shakespare's tragedies the play closes on a note of hope, even assurance. The past seems like a nightmare, and we feel confident that Scotland is now under right direction to be restored 'to a sound and pristine health'.

play the Roman fool i.e. commit suicide.
terms words.
intrenchant unable to be cut. cf. 'trenched', note p.45.
must not is not destined to.
angel In a bad sense – *evil* angel.
upon a pole i.e. on a cloth hung from a pole. At a fair such a notice outside a tent would induce people to go inside and see the 'rare monster'.
unshrinking . . . fought place where he fought without shrinking, or perhaps 'station' may mean 'attitude'.

parted departed, died.
paid his score cf. Ross's words, l.39.
The time is free i.e. men are free once again. cf. the sense of 'time' in Act I Scene v (ten lines from the end); Scene vii, l.81; IV. iii. 70.
pearl i.e. chief nobles.
producing forth bringing forth (to justice).
Scone See note p.38.

Revision questions on Act V

1 Point out the incidents of the play referred to in Lady Macbeth's talking in her sleep.
2 'Some say he's mad'. Do you? Give your reasons.
3 How are the prophecies of the witches fulfilled in this Act?
4 In what spirit does Macbeth meet his end?
5 What is the dramatic value of the succession of short scenes?

Questions

General questions

1 How far is Lady Macbeth's analysis of her husband's character in Act I Scene v justified by subsequent events?

2 Write on the importance of the banquet scene, which occurs about half way through the play.

3 Write a character-sketch of Macbeth, basing your answer upon what Lady Macbeth says of him and to him. Are there any important aspects of his character which she forgets? If so, say how these aspects are revealed.

4 To what extent is Lady Macbeth responsible for the evil deeds of her husband?

5 The murder of Duncan was to give 'solely sovereign sway and masterdom' 'to all our nights and days to come', but it did not turn out like this. Describe the actions of Macbeth after the murder of Duncan in order to maintain his hold upon the throne.

6 Show how the murder of Duncan affected (a) Macbeth (b) Lady Macbeth for the rest of their lives.

7 If you were producing *Macbeth* should you make (a) Lady Macbeth's faint real or pretended, (b) Banquo's ghost appear on the stage? Give your reasons.

8 Describe Macbeth's dealings with the witches and show their influence upon him.

9 Show how Macbeth relies less and less on his wife and more and more on the witches.

10 Do you think that remorse or fear plays the larger part in Macbeth's mental desperation and terror?

11 Trace the downfall of Macbeth from 'worthy gentleman', 'noble Macbeth', to 'this dead butcher'.

12 'Leave all the rest to me.' How is it shown in the play that the task which Lady Macbeth sets herself is too hard for her?

13 Give an account of Lady Macbeth's talk in her sleep, showing what it reveals to the Doctor and the Gentlewoman of her deeds and to us of the memories they had left, even though in a disguised form.

14 Mention any redeeming features in the characters of Macbeth and Lady Macbeth.

15 What is your impression of Banquo (a) *before*, (b) *after* the murder of Duncan? Judge from his own remarks and those of others about him. Do you think that he asked for his fate by not telling anyone what he knew?

16 What do any *two* of the following (i.e. any two of a, b, c, d) contribute to *Macbeth*? (a) The Witches, (b) Macbeth's two interviews with the murderers of Banquo, (c) Macbeth's viewing of the apparitions and the show of eight kings, (d) the conversation between Malcolm and Macduff.

17 Why are any *two* of the following introduced into *Macbeth*? (a) The Porter, (b) Macduff's son, (c) Young Siward. Brief and apt quotation would help.

18 Why are the following in prose? (a) The porter's speech, (b) Lady Macduff's conversation with her little son, (c) Lady Macbeth's talk in her sleep.

19 Express the tragedy of *Macbeth* in one sentence.

20 On the stage *Macbeth* has always been one of the most popular of Shakespeare's plays. Give three reasons which, in your opinion, account for this.

Questions on the text

1 What beast was't then,
That made you break this enterprise to me?
When you durst do it, then you were a man;
And, to be more than what you were, you would
Be so much more the man. Nor time nor place
Did then adhere, and yet you would make both:
They have made themselves, and that their fitness now
Does unmake you.

a) In what way have time and place now 'made themselves'?
b) Is the criticism just that Macbeth is 'unmade'?
c) Put the lines italicized into your own words simply.
d) What does this passage tell us about the character of Lady Macbeth?
e) What had Macbeth just said that called forth Lady Macbeth's antithesis of 'beast'? Point out any other example of antithesis in the passage.

2 Wisdom! to leave his wife, to leave his babes,
His mansion and his titles in a place
From whence himself does fly? He loves us not;
He wants the natural touch: for the poor wren,
The most diminutive of birds, will fight,
Her young ones in her nest, against the owl.
All is the fear, and nothing is the love;
As little is the wisdom, where the flight
So runs against all reason.

a) Do you think that Macduff's flight was 'wisdom' or 'against all reason' – as it would appear before the sequel was known?
b) 'He loves us not.' Would you agree with this?
c) Where did Macduff fly to?
d) What was the next news that he received of his wife and his babes?
e) What is the meaning of 'titles'?
f) Mention any other illustration from birds in the play.

3 *Macbeth.* Thou canst not say I did it: never shake
Thy gory locks at me.
Ross. Gentlemen, rise; his highness is not well.
Lady Macbeth. Sit, worthy friends: my lord is often thus,
And hath been from his youth: pray you, keep seat;
The fit is momentary; upon a thought
He will again be well: if you much note him,
You shall offend him, and extend his passion:
Feed, and regard him not. Are you a man?
Macbeth. Ay, and a bold one, that dare look on that
Which might appal the devil.
Lady Macbeth. O proper stuff!
This is the very painting of your fear:
This is the air-drawn dagger which, you said,
Led you to Duncan.

a) Why was it of particular importance to Lady Macbeth that the banquet should go on?
b) 'Thou canst not say I did it.' To what extent is this true?
c) How did Macbeth occasion the second appearance of Banquo's ghost?

4 Foul whisperings are abroad: unnatural deeds
Do breed unnatural troubles: infected minds
To their deaf pillows will discharge their secrets:
More needs she the divine than the physician:
God, God forgive us all! Look after her;
Remove from her the means of all annoyance,
And still keep eyes upon her: so, good night,
My mind she has mated, and amazed my sight:
I think, but dare not speak.

a) Mention any particular incidents in the play referred to in what Lady Macbeth does or says in this scene whereby she 'discharges her secrets'.
b) What contrasts of feeling are shown in the sleep-walking scene?
c) Who else in the play, at any time, thought 'but dare not speak'?
d) Comment on the two rhyming lines near the end of this passage.

5 'Tis unnatural,
Even like the deed that's done. On Tuesday last,
A falcon, towering in her pride of place,
Was by a mousing owl hawk'd at and kill'd.

a) Mention any other strange occurrence referred to by Ross or the Old Man.
b) Comment on 'On Tuesday last'.
c) What is the *dramatic* reason for these surprising occurrences?
d) In Shakespeare's plays evil omens and unnatural happenings generally attend murders. If you are able, give an example from another play.

6 O worthiest cousin!
The sin of my ingratitude even now
Was heavy on me: thou art so far before,
That swiftest wing of recompense is slow
To overtake thee. Would thou hadst less deserved,
That the proportion both of thanks and payment
Might have been mine! only I have left to say,
More is thy due than more than all can pay.

a) Paraphrase the last four lines.
b) Mention two ways in which Duncan sought to reward Macbeth.
c) Except for the rhyming couplet at the end, this passage is a good example of Shakespeare's later style. Say why, and also say if you consider that there is any reason for the final rhyming couplet.

7 'Tis call'd the evil:
A most miraculous work in this good king;
Which often, since my here-remain in England,
I have seen him do. How he solicits heaven,
Himself best knows: but strangely visited-people,
All swoln and ulcerous, pitiful to the eye,
The mere despair of surgery, he cures;
Hanging a golden stamp about their necks,
Put on with holy prayers: and 'tis spoken,
To the succeeding royalty he leaves
The healing benediction. With this strange virtue,
He hath a heavenly gift of prophecy,
And sundry blessings hang about his throne,
That speak him full of grace.

a) Give another name for 'the evil'.
b) Can you account for the cure?
c) What was the 'golden stamp'?
d) This is a digression from the play. Why do you think that Shakespeare introduces it?
e) What is the meaning here of 'virtue'?
f) 'Since my here-remain in England'. When did Malcolm come to England?

8 *Macbeth.* My dearest love,
Duncan comes here tonight.
Lady Macbeth. And when goes hence?
Macbeth. Tomorrow – as he purposes.
Lady Macbeth. O, never
Shall sun that morrow see!
Your face, my thane, is as a book where men
May read strange matters. To beguile the time,
Look like the time; bear welcome in your eye,

Your hand, your tongue; look like th' innocent flower,
But be the serpent under't. He that's coming
Must be provided for; and you shall put
This night's great business into my dispatch;
Which shall to all our nights and days to come
Give solely sovereign sway and masterdom.
Macbeth. We will speak further.

a) What had been in Lady Macbeth's thoughts before the entrance of her husband here? Quote one or two lines of her speech if you can.
b) Mention any few words typical of Lady Macbeth in her speech printed here.
c) From 'We will speak further' Macbeth is pushed to 'I am settled', two scenes later. Say how.
d) Comment on the last two lines of Lady Macbeth's speech in view of later events of the play.

9 My former speeches have but hit your thoughts,
Which can interpret further: only, I say,
Things have been strangely borne. The gracious Duncan
Was pitied of Macbeth: marry, he was dead:
And the right-valiant Banquo walk'd too late;
Whom, you may say, if't please you, Fleance kill'd,
For Fleance fled: men must not walk too late.
Who cannot want the thought how monstrous
It was for Malcolm and for Donalbain
To kill their gracious father? damned fact!
How it did grieve Macbeth!

a) State briefly the events referred to here.
b) What is peculiar about the way in which they are presented and what is the reason for this?
c) What did Macbeth do as soon as Duncan was found dead?
d) What do we learn from the passage about the loyalties of Lennox?
e) At the end of this speech Lennox discloses that Macduff 'lives in disgrace'. Why?

10 The time has been, my senses would have cool'd
To hear a night-shriek; and my fell of hair

Would at a dismal treatise rouse and stir
As life were in't: I have supp'd full with horrors;
Direness, familiar to my slaughterous thoughts,
Cannot once start me.

a) What *immediate* noise has led Macbeth to these thoughts, and what was his comment when he heard the reason for it?
b) 'The time has been . . .' Of what time is he thinking?
c) Briefly say what the 'horrors' are. Do you think that there is any particular reason why the metaphor 'supp'd' occurs to him?
d) The speech refers to a change which has come over him. What has wrought the change?

11 Knock, knock, knock! Who's there, i' the name of Beelzebub? Here's a farmer that hanged himself on the expectation of plenty: come in time; have napkins enow about you; here you'll sweat for't. (*Knocking within.*) Knock, knock! Who's there, in the other devil's name? Faith, here's an equivocator that could swear in both the scales against either scale; who committed treason enough for God's sake, yet could not equivocate to heaven: O, come in, equivocator. (*Knocking within.*) Knock, knock, knock! Who's there?

a) 'Who's there?' What is the answer?
b) 'Here's a farmer.' 'Here's an equivocator'. What events fresh in the minds of Shakespeare's audience may be alluded to here?
c) Mention any equivocators in the play.
d) Why does the knocking continue so long?
e) At what time of day (or night) is it?
f) What is the speaker probably doing while he is speaking? (This is common stage practice today.)
g) This episode is partly to give an impression of the flight of time. Between what two events?
h) What other dramatic purpose (or purposes) does it serve?
i) Why is the speech in prose? Mention any other scene, or part of a scene, in prose and state the reason.

12 There's comfort yet; they are assailable;
Then be thou jocund: ere the bat hath flown
His cloister'd flight, ere to black Hecate's summons
The shard-borne beetle with his drowsy hums

Hath rung night's yawning peal, there shall be done
A deed of dreadful note.

a) Explain 'jocund', 'cloister'd', 'shard-borne'.
b) To what 'deed' does the speaker refer?
c) What is Shakespeare's purpose in making the imagery suggest night and blackness? Refer to another speech similar in its imagery, not necessarily by the same speaker.
d) For what reason do you think that Hecate is introduced into the play?

Key

1 I. vii. 47–54; **2** IV. ii. 6–14; **3** III. iv. 50–63; **4** V. i. 70–78; **5** II. iv. 10–13; **6** I. iv. 14–21; **7** IV. iii. 141–54; **8** I. v. 56–69; **9** III. vi. 1–11; **10** V. v. 10–15; **11** II. iii. first speech; **12** III. ii. 39–44.

Passages suggested for memorizing

I. iii. 123–6; v. Lady Macbeth's speeches beginning 'Glamis thou art', and 'The raven himself is hoarse'; vii. a few lines here and there from Macbeth's first speech.
III. i. 49–54; ii. 16–26, 46–56; iv. 136–40.
V. iii. 4–10, 20–28; v. 19–28.